THE FORTEAN T

Weird Sex

Dear Steve,
Happy Birthday.
Personally I think the TShirt
is more you!
With love
Kathleen
xxx

To Steve,
Happy Birthday
have a fab time
sweetie, and I
hope you have
a good laugh
while reading
this Book it's
FAB lots of love
Tarla xxx

THE FORTEAN TIMES BOOK OF

Weird Sex

COMPILED BY STEVE MOORE
ILLUSTRATED BY ETIENNE

JOHN BROWN PUBLISHING

First published in Great Britain in September 1995
by John Brown Publishing Ltd, The Boathouse,
Crabtree Lane, Fulham, London SW6 6LU, UK.
Tel 0171 470 2400. Fax 0171 381 3930.

ISBN 1-870870-65-4

Printed and bound in Great Britain by
BPC Paperbacks, Aylesbury.

CONTENTS

Sex. It's everywhere. Even if we're not actually engaged in it, we find it filling up our conversation, our newspapers and books, television and film drama and, of course, those private fantasy worlds that are all our own. Male or female, young or old, we probably spend more time thinking about sex than any other subject in our lives.

Some of us think about sex in very strange ways indeed. Perhaps rather fewer than those who think about weird sex are those who actually indulge in it, and fewer still are those who appear in the newspapers as a result. Less again are those tales which reach the files of Fortean Times, and only a selection of those stories is presented here. As you read through the tales that follow, you might care to consider the vast, seething mass of thoughts, words and deeds that make up the background lying beyond them. If all that thought-sex could be made real, we'd be wading neck-deep in fornication...

Among the stories collected here are some classic tales that have appeared in Fortean Times over the years; the rest are drawn from the sprawling archive we've classified vaguely as "human behaviour". Whether every single tale is entirely true is hard to say, though for the most part we think they are. What's certain is that every one has appeared in print, mainly in newspapers, though occasionally in more learned journals. Although we can't check every case, the best form of guarantee we can offer is to provide our source-references for every tale, which can be found at the end of the book.

Even so, it has to be remembered that in recent years the press (especially the tabloids) has given way to a tendency to print unsubstantiated 'contemporary legends' as if they were fact, with names and dates and places. And journalists, who think about sex no less than the rest of us, occasionally have a tendency to embellish a good story and make it just that little bit better than it really was. These things can't be helped: the stories that follow are presented as we first heard them, and heaven knows some of them are strange enough without further additions.

As always, grateful thanks must go to all those readers and supporters of Fortean Times who've sent us news-clippings over the years, and without whom this book would not have been possible. They're far too numerous to mention, but on this showing they seem to have an obsession with sex and a relish for the perverse which is awesome to behold.

Steve Moore

Embarrassing Accidents

"It seemed like a good idea at the time" must have been the thought occurring to most of the unfortunates in the following tales. It wasn't, of course, and the consequences resulted in red faces (and sometimes other parts of the anatomy) all round.

RETURNING HOME FROM WORKING the night shift in January 1995, an unnamed police officer at Stone, Staffordshire, couldn't resist making passionate advances toward his wife as she was making breakfast. He proceeded to wrap a slice of bread round his penis, at which point his hungry pet labrador took one look at the hot-dog on display and leapt forward for a swift bite. The man, in his twenties, was left rolling on the floor, was off sick for several days, and needed cosmetic surgery. A fellow officer stated that he had been banned from sex for a few weeks, and that everyone was waiting to see how he filled out his sick form. As for the whys and wherefores of the slice of bread, a police spokeswoman remarked: "We couldn't possibly comment on what a police officer does in his spare time." Not in public, anyway...

SPURNED LOVER Marco Zagni of Milan tried to win back his former girlfriend Louisa Pietra in 1987, by swinging Tarzan-style into her bedroom on a rope attached to a pylon. He smashed through the window and knocked himself unconscious. Louisa was unsympathetic. "How could I marry someone so stupid?" she said.

SOUNDING SUSPICIOUSLY like a folktale, we're told that Hans and Rene Deijk of Assen, Holland were at it in the kitchen in December 1994, when Rene had an epileptic fit. This gave her lockjaw at a very delicate moment, leaving Hans to beat his wife about the head with a frying pan in an attempt to get her to open her mouth. Both ended up in hospital: she with head wounds, and he with bites where he'd least like to have them.

NURSES at Princess Margaret Hospital in Swindon bottled out of freeing a man who'd managed to get his penis trapped in a wine bottle in March 1995. The fire brigade were called on to 'uncork' him instead.

UNNAMED, EMBARRASSED and in great pain, a middle-aged man turned up at a fire station in December 1987 with a belt-buckle stuck on his manhood. It became stuck during sex games with his wife at their home in Bristol, and after three hours of tugging at it he asked his son to drive him to the fire station. He arrived with a shopping bag packed with ice wrapped round his member, which by then was badly swollen and turning black. The firemen, unfortunately, were unable to help, and he was taken to Bristol Royal Infirmary, where he was eventually set free by doctors.

It was the other way round for the patient at North Middlesex Hospital in December 1979. In his late twenties, he had a metal ring round his thingie. Doctors decided they were unable to remove the ring, so they called the fire brigade. No less than eleven firemen from the Edmonton station arrived to tackle the problem, armed with hacksaws and compressed air cutters. After two hours they succeeded in freeing the man, using a surgical bone-cutter.

AN EXTREME CASE is that of the 35-year-old man who turned up at Austin Hospital in Melbourne, Australia, in August 1979. He had five steel washers tightly encircling his penis. The medics called in the firemen. The man fainted when the firemen produced bolt-cutters, but recovered and remained conscious during the 45-minute operation to remove the three-quarter inch washers. Despite complaining of considerable pain, he left immediately after the operation without explaining how he got into his predicament.

AMERICAN ARMY officer Major Donald Schneider romantically swept his wife Deborah off her feet to carry her into their hotel room in Fort Leavenworth, Kansas, in November 1989. Unfortunately she was wearing a fur coat, which made her hard to grip, and when she started to fidget he tripped and dropped her over a 3H foot high wooden railing. On the other side was an eight-floor drop into the hotel lobby. Deborah landed on a restaurant table, breaking both legs and her pelvis in the 75 foot fall.

A HARICOT BEAN was regularly used as a plug by a man of 82 having trouble controlling his waterworks. In 1990 the bean got stuck and he tried in vain to remove it with tweezers. After three days it had begun to sprout, so he went to Southend General Hospital in Essex to have it removed with forceps.

WHEN IRAQ ATTACKED ISRAEL during the Gulf War, one of those to suffer was a wife whose cache of passionate letters and intimate pictures of her lover were uncovered when a Scud missile demolished her home. They were found by her husband as he sifted through the rubble. He filed for divorce.

JAZZ TRUMPETER Joe 'Pootie' Newman was a keen ladies' man, and at the age of 66 had surgery for a penile implant. Unfortunately the operation was not a success. A build-up of pressure brought about a series of embarrassing explosions, one of them in a restaurant, and internal bleeding ensued. Three years later, in 1992, he died of a blood clot on the brain.

JUST AS EMBARRASSED, but with less disastrous consequences, was the unnamed man in California, who was fitted with a prototype electronic implant by doctors in 1992. This was designed to help impotent men rise to the occasion by remote control. Unfortunately, the 52-year-old patient got a lift every time his neighbours used their electronic car doors.

A DRUNKEN NIGHT OF PASSION came to a climax in July 1990 when a brunette allowed her boyfriend to paint her from head to toe in yacht varnish. The finishing touch was added when he made her wear a dog collar as well. The trouble began the next morning, when she tried to scrub off her gloss finish. Unable to remove it and still wearing the dog collar, she headed off to her local hospital in Gillingham, Kent, in search of help. When asked how she had got into her predicament, she turned shy and vanished. Fearing she was a fire risk in that condition, doctors informed the police who eventually tracked her down and returned her to the hospital, where the varnish was finally removed.

A PENSIONER'S TESTICLES got trapped between the slats of a patio chair in May 1994 after he took a shower at his home in Eastbourne. The fire brigade tried grease and other lubricants to help Ron Tupper, but only finally freed him after an hour by using cutting equipment to demolish the chair.

ROBERT CHEUVRONT, 33, took a very early morning dip in a motel pool in Lakeland, Florida, in July 1994. He was trapped in the shallow end for three hours after getting his penis stuck in the suction filter. How he achieved this is not explained, but it was only at 4.45am that a night clerk heard his cries for help. His swollen penis was eventually extricated by an ambulance crew using lubricants.

A NAKED COUPLE'S tree-top love-making was inter-rupted when the woman plunged from the branches and broke her leg. Elizabeth Hooper, 29, and Jeff Healey, 35, had crept into Windsor Great Park for an all-night romp on 2 August 1994, choosing an oak tree close to the cavalry training grounds for their arboreal encounter. Jeff shinned down, dressed hastily and went for help, leaving barmaid and ex-strippergram Elizabeth stark naked and in agony, to be found by a Crown Estates ranger. She was taken to Wexham Park Hospital in Slough, where she was later discharged after being caught having sex in a busy ward with an unnamed man.

HANS MEYER, 35, spread a blanket in the boot of his BMW and climbed in with a female companion, in May 1994. During their love-making, the boot slammed shut, locking them in. Fortunately, Meyer had his mobile phone with him, and managed to call police at Erlenbach, Germany. They eventually freed the pair, but only after being persuaded that the phone call was not a joke.

DUTCH FIREMEN had to be called to the rescue of a man in the Hague who found himself trapped in handcuffs after sex games with a prostitute backfired, in December 1991. The prostitute manacled the man at his own request, but was unable to free him afterwards, and the firemen had to use bolt-cutters to release him.

CHARNCHAI PUANMUANGPAK was 13 years old and addicted to the Thai perversion known as 'pumping'. Most pumpers use a bicycle pump, inserting the nozzle into their rectum and giving themselves a rush of air, but Charnchai decided to go further. He moved on to a two-cylinder foot-pump and then, egged on by schoolfriends, decided he was going to try the compressed air hose at a nearby petrol station. In August 1993 he sneaked in under cover of darkness: not realising how powerful the machine was, he inserted the tube into his body, put a coin in the slot, and was killed almost instantly.

AN UNNAMED 34-year-old man in New York squirted a cocaine solution into his urethra to heighten his sexual pleasure in June 1987. Immediately after intercourse with his girlfriend he suffered a persistent painful erection which lasted three days before he sought medical help. Soon afterwards he developed blood clots in his genitals, arms and legs, back and chest. After 12 days in hospital, gangrene had set in, and he ended up losing both his legs, nine fingers and his penis.

IN JULY 1980, the *British Medical Journal* carried a short report headed "penile injuries from vacuum cleaners". While the authors, from London hospitals, were of the opinion that penis and vacuum cleaner had been brought together "in search of sexual excitement", the excuses offered by the patients were rather different. One man of 60 said that he was changing the plug of the vacuum in the nude while his wife was out shopping. It suddenly "turned itself on" and caught his penis, causing deep lacerations. A 65-year-old railway signalman was in his signal box when he bent down to pick up his tools and caught his penis in the vacuum "which happened to be switched on." And a man of 49 was vacuuming his friend's staircase in a loose-fitting dressing gown when, intending to switch the machine off, he leaned across to reach the plug: "At that moment his dressing gown became undone and his penis was sucked into the vacuum cleaner." The men were using a brand of cleaner with fan-blades only 15 centimetres from the inlet; their wounds were repaired by doctors, leaving only minor scarring.

There is worse, however: a 57-year-old American man was found dead, slumped over a vacuum cleaner in 1988. He was naked with his testicles, thighs and buttocks bound with panty hose. Also at the scene was a bottle of wine, a glass of urine, jars of lubricant and a faeces-laden wooden table leg. The sound of a vacuum cleaner running for a very long time tipped off a neighbour. Cause of death was a heart attack.

APPALLING AND ASTONISHING as the next tale may be, it's impeccably documented in a medical journal for 1991. An unmarried loner in Pennsylvania worked in a machine shop and remained behind when his colleagues went to lunch. Finding himself alone he began the regular practice of masturbating by holding his penis against the canvas drive belt of a large piece of machinery. One day, as he approached orgasm, he lost his concentration and leaned too close to the belt. His scrotum suddenly became caught between the pulley-wheel and the drive-belt and he was thrown into the air, landing a few feet away. Unaware that he had lost his left testicle, and too stunned to feel much pain, he closed the wound with a heavy-duty staple-gun and resumed work. Several days later, the eight staples went rusty and his scrotum, now black, red and blue, had swollen to twice the size of a grapefruit and was oozing blood and pus. Only at this point did the man go to see a doctor. Those repairs that were possible were made, and the man left hospital within a week. As the doctor writing the report remarked: "I can only assume he abandoned this method of self-gratification."

Thanks for the Mammaries

Big or small, they obsess men everywhere... and quite a few women as well. There are so many of these tales that at times it's hard to keep abreast of them, but here we uncover a few choice reports...

AT ABOUT TWO in the morning on a September Sunday in 1988, two Texan women were bragging over CB radio about which of them had the more amply developed bosom. They agreed to meet in the parking lot at Truck Stops of America in Mesquite, a suburb of Dallas. When the women arrived, one grabbed a tyre iron and struck the other five times. Her victim seized a hammer from her truck and began defending herself. Both women suffered cuts and bruises; the first was arrested for aggravated assault and the other was treated in Mesquite Community Hospital and later released. The news report failed to mention which of the ladies had the larger breasts and the case didn't come to court, but the incident was the talk of Mesquite for weeks afterwards.

TOPLESS GO-GO DANCER Morgana Roberts was arrested for invading a baseball pitch during a game in April 1985. Protesting her innocence, she blamed the law of gravity, saying that she leaned over a fence to get a better view, at which point her 60-inch chest just toppled her over. Her lawyer told the court: "Seven out of ten times if you lean her over a rail she topples over it."

DANCER 'CHESTY LOVE' (real name Cynthia Hess) persuaded Judge Joan Pate in April 1994 that her breast operation was an allowable business expense for tax purposes, winning a three-year battle. She was claiming $2,088 for surgical implants that ballooned her bust size to a gargantuan 56FF, which, as the judge remarked, "contorted her body into a grotesque appearance, all for the purpose of making money." It worked too. Dancing as 'Tonda Marie' before the implants, she grossed $750 a week; afterwards her income swelled to $3,000 a week.

Judge Pate ruled that Hess's breasts, which weigh about 10 pounds each, could only be considered as business assets, rather than objects of personal benefit to her. It was also pointed out that they make her appear freakish, her family has stopped talking to her, passers-by laugh, she overbalances easily, and she hasn't seen her feet since the operation.

IN MERRIFIELD, Virginia, Bruce Henri worked as a mail sorter – until 1992, when he complained to his boss that a colleague's big breasts were distracting him. She was walking around with several of her blouse buttons undone, and 42-year-old Henri said: "She was exposing a lot of cleavage and if she was wearing a bra it was one of those lift-up things that provide enhancement. To me, it was very distracting and inappropriate for a woman to expose her breasts this way in front of fellow workers. You've got to think right to sort mail properly." Henri was sent home while an investigation was carried out, where he remained for the next two years, drawing £32,000 wages without doing a stroke of work.

A GOGGLE-EYED DRIVER at Plympton, Devon, lost his concentration in May 1987 when a tall, slim blonde wiggled across the road in front of him. She was wearing only a mini-skirt and a pair of high-heeled shoes. The driver swerved and flattened a traffic bollard, then called the police. They arrived just in time to see the girl disappearing into nearby woods, but when they reached the spot all they found were her stilettos, embedded in a grass verge. A highly enthusiastic police search ensued, which lasted until the following day and included the use of a helicopter. No trace of the girl was found.

EQUALLY DISTRACTING is the topless robbery trick, which seems to work over and over again. In Salisbury, Wiltshire, a blonde woman in her thirties walked into three successive clothing shops in September 1986. The well-endowed woman was wearing a skirt and wrap-over top, which she opened to bare her breasts. While staff and shoppers goggled in surprise, her male companion walked round the racks helping himself. From the three shops they netted ten suits, 11 women's dresses and a number of sweaters, worth more than £3,000.

IN MAY 1988, police in the German city of Cologne were reporting a sudden increase in tourists falling prey to girls who bared their breasts and then stole their wallets. "The girls either rip open their shirts or hoist their skirts, then grab the wallet in the confusion and run off," said a police spokesman. "We don't quite know what to do about it."

DUTCH SUPERMARKETS were the target of a series of raids by a gang that included six "busty young women". The girls would rush in and start to strip in time to gipsy music from a cassette player, and their male accomplices would rifle the tills while everyone's attention was distracted. They carried out a string of successful raids from February 1994 onwards. Witnesses could not give a full description of the topless bandits, possibly because they were paying little attention to anything above the shoulders. They were eventually brought to book in June, when hard-boiled owner Albert Goorman hit the alarm button as soon as they began displaying their wares in his supermarket at Deventer.

A GANG of Thai transvestites robbed tourists in December 1992 by enticing them to suck their tranquilliser-laced nipples, sending them to sleep. Four transvestites and a woman were arrested in Bangkok after complaints from a Syrian and a Hong Kong man, who were robbed of a Rolex watch and nearly £2,000 in cash. The gang told police they adopted the ploy because "many customers did not drink".

AFTER A 1994 TEST-CASE involving a group of women, a court ruled that it's permissible (although perhaps not advisable) for women to ride the New York subway topless – so long as they don't panhandle, smoke or chew gum, all of which remain illegal.

HYPNOTIST Steve Marek from Lexington, Virginia, found himself the subject of a lawsuit brought by the Kentucky attorney general in May 1994. He had run a series of newspaper adverts claiming that he could help women develop larger breasts through the power of suggestion. One's tempted to ask what sort of suggestions he was making. The lawsuit was brought on the grounds that he would be unable to deliver on his promises.

DAVID WILCOX, a 25-year-old policeman from Florida, frisked dozens of women drivers, claiming he was hunting a suspect with a tattooed nipple. In May 1993 he quit the force after admitting he had a breast fetish.

AN APPLICATION to open a topless barber shop in Austin, Texas, was turned down by the State Board of Barber Examiners in July 1985. The shop was to have been staffed entirely by young women who would have specialised in shaves. It was turned down as unsanitary, with the remark that "a hair'll work under the skin of the barber and can grow up to five or six feet inside the body". However, it seems there might have been some room for manoeuvre if the young ladies concerned could have found a way to sterilize their bodies after every customer.

THE REVEREND Louis Hillendahl, 56, of Ingleside, Illinois, was granted a leave of absence by the United Methodist Church in February 1977. He had been conducting nude breast-feeding therapy sessions with his parishioners, and planned to write a book about the experiments, which dealt with the concept of "sexuality as a myth perpetrated onto man". The therapy experiments involved unrelated men, women and children above the age of eight. Most of the sessions were held in the summer of 1975, but one Ingleside housewife said she had continued to nurse the minister and his wife, Mary Lou, 55, until the summer of the following year.

A YOUNG MOTHER was charged with sexual abuse and jailed in Syracuse, NY, in December 1992, after asking innocently whether it was normal to experience arousal while nursing her child.

LI XIAOMO, one of a number of 'hairy people' born in China, was covered with thick, glossy, black hair all over, except for her palms and soles. She also had two enormous extra breasts, each weighing nearly 22 pounds, which were surgically removed in 1980.

Tackle Tales

It's the ambition of most men to be fine and upstanding, but there are some fairly abnormal ways of going about the matter – as these tales of penile dementia testify

LONG-DISTANCE LORRY DRIVER Alpha Mussika was addicted to the African drug *khat*, chewing it all day long. The Dar-es-Salaam trucker visited his doctor in 1992 wearing rubber incontinence pants and complaining that he had been ejaculating more than 40 times a day for the previous month. A week later he suffered total erection failure, and though he abstained from khat completely for the following nine months, he remained impotent. His doctor was reported as saying she believed he had used up his entire lifetime's supply of orgasms in that one month.

IN KUALA LUMPUR, an unnamed man paid 20 Malaysian dollars for sex with 26-year-old prostitute Vasanthy Rahman in 1994 and took her to a local hotel. Undressing, he revealed that he had had two small ball-bearings inserted into the tip of his penis to increase his pleasure. Apparently this procedure is not uncommon in Malaysia, but when Ms

Rahman saw what he had to offer, she screamed and beat him unconscious with a broom, breaking his left forearm in the process. Failing even to get his money refunded, the man took Rahman to court on charges of theft and assault. The judge sentenced her to one day's imprisonment.

THE CHIEF SURGEON at the Cincinatti Shriners Burns Institute was sacked in 1992 for drawing happy faces on the manhood of two patients "to relieve stress". He had also carved his initials on the skull of a child during an operation.

MORE CURIOUS is the case of the man arrested for exposing himself to two girls on a bus in South Yorkshire in 1990. The girls reported to the police, and independently described the man as having a tattoo on his penis. Within five minutes, the police had taken the girls back to the scene, where they identified a young man as the flasher. He denied the offence but admitted having a tattoo in the relevant place. Nonetheless, when he was prosecuted for indecent exposure, the magistrates acquitted him. The prosecutor, commenting on the case, pointed out that magistrates were entitled to use their local knowledge in judging a case, and said: "I can only conclude that tattooing one's penis must be a common practice in the area".

HOAXERS in China were said to be cashing in on the traditional Chinese preference for boy babies in 1988, by attaching false male genitals to girls and selling them to gullible peasants. The official New China News Agency reported that a couple in Hebei province, who had three daughters but desperately wanted a son and heir, paid a dealer £300 for a 'boy'. The false genitals dropped off a week later.

WORRYING STATISTICS revealed by London urologist Ronald Miller in August 1994 showed that up to 200 men a year break their penises during lovemaking. In most cases the woman is on top when both lovers hear a loud crack, and the man is left needing up to 40 stitches and a splint. One such sufferer was Wolfgang Emmerhe of Stuttgart, who claimed on his insurance under an "accidental collision" clause. When the company refused to pay in March 1995, he took them to court, where he was awarded £1,300 for repairs.

There are less happy endings, though. A surgeon in Munich made a 42-year-old man's bent penis even wonkier by inserting an implant the wrong way round in January 1995. A second operation failed as well, leaving him unable to make love to his 28-year-old wife. Twenty other patients were said to have complained about the same surgeon.

THE MEN OF KENYA were warned in October 1992 against the practice of washing their genitals with battery acid after sex, as a preventative against Aids. A doctor said the end result could be "even more disastrous".

AN EQUALLY UNPLEASANT case from December 1994 concerns the wife of Giorgio Forti, 32, who took revenge by slipping ground pepper into his condoms before he left to visit his mistress. He was later rushed to a Rome hospital, suffering from severe swelling and inflammation.

AN AUSTRALIAN WOMAN who worked for the Federal Community Services and Health Department in Adelaide claimed sickness benefits for stress, and said that she and her husband, the office supervisor, had been made physically and mentally ill by a furry toy penis kept in a plastic cage on top of a filing cabinet by a female colleague. The toy first appeared in February 1989, and the woman left work in August that year; after which she received £6,000 in rehabilitation expenses, including counselling, gymnasium membership and money for an interior decorating course. Her husband had received £17,000 in benefits for anxiety and depression. In April 1991, the woman lost her claim for further sickness benefits.

In a similar tale of excess, in 1995 a London firm was ordered to pay £4,500 to a secretary after she told a tribunal that her boss had eaten a chocolate penis at a Christmas lunch.

GERMAN MEN were reported to be flying across the Atlantic in 1994 to have two inches surgically added to their penises. One US clinic alone was said to have carried out 1,500 such operations in the previous 18 months.

FEELING CERTAIN that American doctors never believed claims of new cures, London doctor Professor Giles Brindley, 59, exposed himself to 40 men and women to prove his treatment for impotency actually worked. Before his lecture to the American Urological Association in Las Vegas in 1986, he injected himself with enough of his new drug to give himself an erection for an hour. Then, when the conference chairman asked for evidence, down came the trousers.

AN ISRAELI undergoing treatment for impotence in November 1994 was taken to hospital after a serum he injected at home gave him a 36-hour erection. While doctors at the hospital were used to seeing patients with a four-hour erection, they hadn't come across anything like this before. The condition was alleviated by drawing blood from the penis, and the man was allowed home after a three-day stay.

A MORE RADICAL CURE for impotence was reported from China in 1986. Surgeons in Shanghai were said to have developed a technique whereby muscle was transplanted from the patient's arms to strengthen or rebuild their penises. It was claimed that two patients successfully treated in this way had become fathers. British doctors remained sceptical.

DAOIST MONK Chan Tze-Tan of Hong Kong demonstrated his mastery of the art of Qi-Gong in February 1995 by lifting 72lb with his penis. The 49-year-old father of five roped the weight to his penis and lifted it six inches off the ground, then swung it back and forth between his legs eight times.

TOURISTS TRAVELLING to New Guinea were warned in April 1994 that they could have their penises pulled as a sign of goodwill. In a remote area of Irian Jaya it is apparently considered a friendly gesture, and one that should not be misconstrued.

POLICE IN MALAGA, Spain, were alerted in November 1992 by a woman who said she had been held prisoner in a car for four hours by a man with two penises, who obliged her to perform fellatio. She was quite certain about her assailant's distinguishing characteristics. For two weeks the police tried to trace the vehicle, but then switched to questioning medics and found the culprit in an instant. He was named as José Lopez, 26, who was positively identified and then released. No one seems to know why they let him go.

CHAPTER THREE

AT DOBBIGAN, in Yuro County, California, a cult known as the Church of the ABC of Abraham erected a rather startling monument in May 1995. The cult is led by one Caligula Croesus Spurtyn which, astonishingly, is his original name and appears on his birth certificate. Made of Sicilian marble and dappled with veins of Corsican jasper, the 244 foot high, 57 foot circumference pillar is a replica of Spurtyn's penis. The replica is also topped by an eternal flame which, one rather suspects, is probably not present in the original. Shortly afterwards, a Mexican restaurant owned by the cult was shut down when it was discovered that one of the condiments used there was Spurtyn's semen.

CHAPTER FOUR

Bobbitted

When Lorena Bobbitt took a knife to her
husband John's pecker in 1993, she started
what has become the archetypal penis
severing tale. But her story was hardly
the first, and only one among an
extraordinary number...

A CHINESE HOUSEWIFE, acting on the advice of a
soothsayer in 1994, cut off her husband's penis while he
slept in the belief that he would grow a new one which
would restore their marriage.

Equally strange is the tale of the Cambodian woman living in Sydney, Australia. In October 1985 she was tried for
maliciously wounding her five-year-old son, after cutting off
his penis in the belief that it held the spirit of her estranged
husband. Surgeons managed to reattach the organ.

A RATHER DIFFERENT TWIST turns up in the tale of
Cynthia Mason Gillett, 28, of Waynesville, North Carolina.
In July 1993 she doused her sleeping husband's penis with

nail-polish remover and set fire to it. Gursham Gillett, 27, refused to testify against his wife, whose motives for the attack remained unknown, and so she merely received probation.

THE APTLY NAMED ROGER COX, 35, cut off his penis in March 1982 and, as his wife joined him in prayer, threw it on the fire at his home in Saron, near Denbigh, Wales. The father of eight said he did it so he could devote all his time to preaching, which he did from a double-decker bus. His wife said that they had discussed the act for 12 years, and that her husband's justification was Matthew 19:12: "...and there are eunuchs who have made themselves eunuchs for the sake of the Kingdom of Heaven."

PLUMBER Cyprian Okech had his private parts hacked off by witch-doctors in Uganda in 1986, but was too drunk to notice. His attackers also tried to cut out his tongue, but he was rescued by police and taken to hospital in Kampala. The organs would have been used in black magic rituals.

In a parallel but reverse case, we hear of a 30-year-old 'Satanist' from Munich, Germany, who cut off his penis with a blunt knife in 1994. He was about to mutilate his testicles when the police arrived and stopped him... which leaves us wondering: how did the cops know?

IN SOUTH AFRICA, Kallie Fortuin, 19, raped an old lady in 1981 and was caught riding her bicycle the next day by her son and his friend. At gunpoint they took him to a remote riverbank, gave him a knife used to castrate pigs, and told him it was either snip it or snuff it. Without books, training or anaesthetics, he did the job, and the men then took him to a police station. When he was tried for rape,

Fortuin told the court he had seen pigs castrated and knew what to do, and a doctor confirmed he had made a neat job of it. Retribution already having been carried out, Fortuin avoided hanging and got 10 years; the lady's relatives were simply warned not to take the law into their own hands again.

A MALAYSIAN MAN of 27 had his penis bitten off by a tortoise after taking a swim in a pool near Batu Arang in 1983. A search of the pool proved fruitless, and he ended up recuperating in hospital in Kuala Lumpur.

LIVERPOOL POLICE found a man wearing only a jacket wandering on the M62 motorway at Bowring Park in September 1986. The 49-year-old married man's penis had been cut off, and he said he had been attacked in a field by two men, stripped and mutilated. He was taken to hospital, where he later confessed that he did it himself.

Conversely, Ahmet Samanci cut off his penis with a butcher's knife in 1991 to end rumours that he was chasing his neighbour's wife in the Turkish town of Usak. The 64-year-old grandfather was heard by neighbours shouting "I am an honourable man!"

A BREADKNIFE was used by Heidi Siebke, 51, to cut off her boyfriend's penis after a drunken row in October 1992. She said Hans-Joachim Kampioni, 56, continually pestered her for sex and, defending herself, she knocked him out with a stool. Then she went to work with the knife, and tried to cover her tracks by setting fire to his house in Frankfurt-an-der-Oder. The penis was damaged in the blaze and could not be reattached, so Kampioni auctioned it in a local pub for £40 and a bottle of schnapps. "It's no use to me any more," he said. "I have to go to the toilet like a woman, and when I see a pretty girl, nothing stirs." Heidi was jailed for three years.

Also making the best of it was Lonnie Destry of New Orleans, who lost both testicles while using a chainsaw to cut logs. When doctors failed to reattach them, he had them preserved in glass and used them as a paperweight.

MORE PATHETIC is the tale of Kevin Baker, who prefers to be known as Laura. The 36-year-old father of four was told he would have a three-year wait for a sex-change operation, but he was going blind from glaucoma and was desperate to see himself as a woman. So in July 1994 he attempted to do it himself, with a razor-blade. He failed to complete the operation before his screams alerted his wife, who duly called the emergency services. They took him away to hospital where, rather unfairly it seems, his penis was reattached. Baker said he'd try again, but using a machete, so he could get it all over with in one blow.

A BETTING FRENZY overtook San Felice, southern Italy, in February 1995, after reports that a jilted mistress had bitten her lover's penis. Many Italians use a curious system to fill in the weekly lottery by assigning a special significance to each number, so in this case they rushed to put their money on 29, said to symbolize sex.

IN A CASE OF PRUDERY GONE MAD, Sicilian priest Father Salvatore Zappala decided to put underpants on four marble statues of angels round the high altar of his church at Calatabiano in 1983. "I felt they were indecent," he said. A puzzling statement, as angels normally have no private parts in the first place.

A Walk On The Wild Side

Things are not always what they seem, and neither are people. Regardless of their original sex, transvestites and transsexuals occupy centre stage in the following tales...

LET US BEGIN with a tale from long ago about a woman named Hamilton from Taunton, Somerset. In the 1740s she posed as a man and married 14 wives in succession. After each marriage she dumped the unfortunate bride, pocketed her dowry, then made off and proposed to someone else. Eventually the law caught up with her, but no one was sure what to do with her: as marriages between women weren't legal, she could hardly be charged with bigamy. In the end she appeared at Taunton Assizes in 1746 accused of being "a common nuisance and disturber of the peace", and was sentenced to be publicly whipped.

ROSALINDA DE HERNANDEZ, of Tegucigalpa, Honduras, had more than one shock coming in August 1987. Not only was her 'husband' Gustavo killed in a bar-room fight with a woman, but Gustavo turned out to be actually female, too... and six months pregnant besides. Rosalinda, who had been married to Gustavo for nine years, said that although their love-life had seemed odd, she had never suspected her husband was a woman.

CHEYEN WEATHERLY spent eight days at the Coronado High School in Colorado Springs in 1990, and made it onto the cheerleading squad, in spite of being 5ft 9in tall and 164 pounds. She said she was 17 years old and a transfer student from Greece, and several football players expressed an interest in dating her. 'She' turned out eventually to be Charles Janloyames Daugherty, 26, with a record of theft, shoplifting, burglary and criminal impersonation. He was also said to have multiple personalities, and had been caught impersonating a cheerleader for a minor-league football team the year before. Betsy Acree, who led that cheerleading squad, said: "She was great...I have nothing bad to say about the girl, except she wasn't a girl." Daugherty got two years' probation.

BUDDHIST NUN Chei Fui was a demure and humble member of a religious community near Taipei, Taiwan, admired for her devoutness by her fellow nuns. Then in 1986, after 14 years as a member of the community, Chei Fui was surprised by the abbess while taking a bath in the middle of the night. It was quite clear that 'she' should have been a monk all along, but as she'd never misbehaved in any way, it was decided that she could stay where she was.

JAZZ MUSICIAN Billy Tipton died in 1989, aged 74, after an honourable career as saxophone and piano player with the likes of the Jack Teagarden and Scott Cameron bands, before forming the Billy Tipton Trio in 1951 and playing nightclubs throughout western America. Married to nightclub entertainer Kitty Oakes for 18 years and raising three adopted sons, it was only when Tipton died that it was revealed that the 'regular guy' was a woman. He had apparently told his wife that a car accident had left him unable to have sex, so they slept in separate beds and Tipton always wore pyjamas.

LIVING IN LISBON happily enough for 18 years, General Tito Anibal de Paixao Gomes borrowed from his neighbours against his military pension until 1992, when the highly-decorated war veteran went on trial for fraud and failing to repay £11,000 in loans. It turned out that the 'general' had never been in the military, and a medical examination revealed his true identity: Maria Teresinha da Jesus Gomes, a woman of 60 who had disappeared from the island of Madeira after a broken romance. She had hired a general's uniform for a carnival in 1975, and then met Joaquina de Conceicao, a retired nurse and widow 15 years her senior. They married and went to Lisbon, where it was five years before Joaquina discovered her husband's true sex when she wandered into the bathroom one day.

PERHAPS THE LONGEST PRETENCE was that of Gerrard Mohapi, born in Lesotho, South Africa, who died in 1986 at the age of 85. For the previous 30 years he had been known as "Nurse Christina", and it was only after death that the nurse was discovered to be a man. Under one name or another, he had masqueraded as a woman for 70 years.

THE COLONIAL INHABITANTS of New York were amazed in 1702 to see their governor, Lord Cornbury, open the state assembly on behalf of Queen Anne, wearing a hooped skirt and head-dress and carrying a fan. "You stupid people," he told those who gasped. "I represent a woman and I ought to do so as faithfully as I can." Soon afterwards he adopted women's dress at all times, at which point he was sent back to England, probably to the great relief of all concerned.

A STRANGER TALE YET from 1908. Beatrice Alger, 24, was arrested at Chingford, for the felony (as it then was) of being a man disguised as a woman. When arrested he was wearing women's clothes, but his defence counsel explained that he had been brought up as a girl and always wore women's clothing. Until his arrest he had always believed that he was woman. The court believed that he had no intention of disguising himself and jailed him for one day; which meant that, as he had been held on remand, he was immediately released.

A PAKISTANI TAXI DRIVER, named only as H. Khan, disguised himself in a woman's gown and veil to visit his married lover in the Gulf emirate of Ras al-Khaimah. He was given away when he removed his veil inside the house, and the woman's children informed their father that their mother's visitor had a big moustache. In August 1992 Khan got 60 lashes and four months in jail; the woman got 90 lashes and 18 months jail.

TRANSPORT CORPS Private Patrick Smallwood, 22, was arrested in February 1990 after crashing his car through a boutique window and stealing a £225 evening gown. When caught, the 6ft 3in tall soldier was found wearing the off-the-shoulder gold lame dress, fishnet stockings, red suspenders and high-heeled shoes. He was fined £500, and an army witness told the court that his military prospects were "limited".

AN EXETER WELDER made a bad mistake when he pulled a screaming blonde into a cemetery in 1987. Stephen Flockton's victim turned out to be a man in drag, who beat him off by biting his finger and lashing out with his high-heeled shoes. Flockton, 22, was charged with attempted indecent assault.

In contrast, a transvestite mugger wearing big false breasts and a tartan skirt attacked a 16-year-old girl as she walked home in Nottingham in 1988. She screamed and grappled with him, at which point the man hoisted his skirts and ran off empty-handed.

SEX-CHANGE OPERATIONS are reasonably common-place these days, but some curious tales still turn up. Two French brothers became sisters in 1992: Patrick and Yannick Paton both had sex changes and became known as Dominique and Alix.

Not to be outdone, three Chinese sisters from Henan province all had sex changes, the last being the youngest, a 14-year-old who had her operation in February 1993.

CHINESE SURGEONS PERFORMED the first direct sex-swap operation in 1992, when a 22-year-old woman exchanged her ovaries for a 30-year-old man's testicles. A penis was constructed for the woman from her stomach lining, while the man received a vagina made of leather. Both hope to marry, but neither will be able to reproduce. "The man thinks that women are clean and men are dirty," said a doctor. "The woman thinks that it's better for her career to be a man."

JANEEN NEWMAN and David Willis lived together in Louth, Lincolnshire, but were refused a normal marriage, because Janeen was formerly John, a Grimsby trawlerman, and David had been a woman with an eight-year-old daughter. Under British law, it is possible to marry only as the gender on your birth certificate; they were advised they could only marry if Mr Willis agreed to take Miss Newman as his "lawful wedded husband", while she'd have to take him as her "wife".

SERIAL KILLER David Berkowitz, otherwise known as "Son of Sam", who terrorised New York for a year and killed five women and a man, was reported in 1981 to have fallen in love with a sex-change jailmate. Berkowitz, 28 at the time, fell for 25-year-old Louis "Diane" Quirros, an armed robber who was moved to a nearby cell. Quirros had been allowed hormone treatment to enlarge his breasts, but had been refused a full sex-change operation. When Berkowitz's feelings were discovered, they were parted.

CHAPTER SIX

Flash Harries (& Harriets)

While many of us have a tendency to show off, some folks take it further than others, revealing, if not everything, at least the important parts. And it's not just men, either...

STRUTTING down London's Charing Cross Road in 1984, Edwin Johnson whipped open his full-length fur coat and exposed himself first to two men, then a teenage girl, and finally to two plainclothes policemen, who duly arrested him. Nothing so unusual about that, except that Johnson, naked under the coat, had no genitalia whatsoever to expose. He had recently undergone a sex-change operation, and also called himself Linda Gold.

At the police station, (s)he was charged under both names, and when it came to the matter of sex, a question mark was put down on the charge sheet. As women can't be charged with indecent exposure, Johnson, 21, was charged with insulting behaviour. Asked if he had anything further to say, he flashed at the station sergeant. He was fined £25.

DEREK GILL, 55, appeared in a Wolverhampton court in November 1990. He had been arrested while walking around wearing nothing but a coat over his shoulders and a Lone Ranger-type mask, on which was written a message referring to his "naked Tonto". The aforesaid Tonto was tied to a blue cord which then went round Gill's neck, making the thing wobble about when he moved his head. Gill was said to be a keen naturist, and it was claimed in court that he was walking naked to relieve an irritating skin condition. Curiously, it was also revealed that Gill had been banned from several naturist clubs because of his "unusual dress sense".

A MINNEAPOLIS MAN was charged with indecent exposure in May 1992 after a car chase which caused several collisions. When the car was stopped, the 37-year-old was found to be naked from the waist downwards, with four $1 bills attached to his penis. Police said they had picked him up several times before, naked but with higher-denomination bills attached.

A HOUSE FULL OF GIRL STUDENTS in Chester was an inviting target for Robin Pugh, 31. Having already been seen standing naked on a wall and showing himself off to two girls, his big moment came at 1am one night in May 1986. One of the girls heard a rattle at the front door and went downstairs to see his face pressed against the glass. His privates were stuck through the letter box, a position that he managed to keep up for almost an hour. He was put on 12 months' probation.

IN BRUSSELS, Harold De Notte, 38, was known as the "Devil in a Dirty Mac". When finally arrested in 1990, he claimed that he had exposed himself to 1,500 women, and proudly told Belgian police: "I've been doing it four times a week for eight years. The only time I stopped was during my summer holiday with my wife and kids." At the same time, Brussels police were also searching for another flasher who painted his privates green and orange.

A CYCLIST at Corby, Northants, flashed at or indecently assaulted 40 women between 1984 and 1987. He wore stockings and suspenders and, in a cunning form of disguise, used different coloured bicycles.

A NAKED MAN was arrested in August 1988, for dancing daily at noon in a cemetery. The unemployed farm-hand from Biassa, Italy, had to be protected from furious widows by police. He said: "It was the only pleasure I had in life."

IN SEPTEMBER and October 1986, Timothy Adrian Ward, 32, exposed himself to women horseriders near his home in Middlesbrough. At the time he wore a full-length rubber wet-suit, a gas mask, and had two hot water bottles dangling on a piece of string round his neck. When he was arrested at Thornton-le-Beans, near Northallerton, police found wet-suit, gas mask, hot water bottles, rubber gauntlets, two pairs of wellingtons, a pair of cut-off waders and a yellow rubber coat in his car. He was prosecuted in court, fined £250 and had his gas mask confiscated.

IT WAS, PERHAPS, A MISTAKE to give 'Gipsy Joe' a one-piece, police-issue paper suit before leading him into court in Shepton Mallet to answer a charge of "lewdly expos-ing himself to women" in July 1992. No sooner had the 50-year-old, who refused to give his real name, been asked if he understood the charge than he tore open the front of the suit and produced 'Exhibit A'.

"Do you find this offensive?" he asked the three magistrates, one of whom was a woman. Before they could answer, he turned to show his evidence to the ladies in the public gallery as well. As he was led away to the cells he spat on the floor and shouted: "This court is cursed by Gipsy Joe." The magistrates were not amused, but a policeman had to leave the court because he couldn't control his laughter.

VALERIE MORALES, 27, began an interesting chain of events when she went walking, stark naked, along a Los Angeles street at dawn in May 1988. Two distracted car drivers crashed at the sight of her, whereupon an ambulance was summoned, to find that, in the meantime, Morales had decided to lie down beside the accident. Finding a nude woman in the road, the paramedics naturally loaded her into the ambulance before treating the drivers for minor injuries. They then looked round to discover that Morales had driven off in their vehicle. She proceeded to drive the wrong way down a freeway until she crashed into a bread truck. Fleeing on foot, still naked, she was pursued and captured by a sheriff's deputy who happened to be driving past at the time, transporting a van full of prisoners. She was arrested on charges of stealing the ambulance and driving while under the influence of drink or drugs; her nudity doesn't seem to have been taken into account at all.

APPARENTLY THINKING that she had run out of petrol on the Santa Ana Freeway in Los Angeles, a 38-year-old woman stood on the bonnet of her Plymouth station wagon, pulled her dress over her hips, threw money in the air and whacked oncoming cars with a chrome chain to which her keys were fastened. Perhaps distracted by the fact that she wasn't wearing any underwear, commuters ran in circles chasing the money, while not noticing that the notes were torn in half. A mile-long traffic jam built up that morning in April 1989, until finally someone used their car phone to summon the police. When they arrived, they found plenty of petrol in the car, at which point the woman said she was a prostitute and needed attention. She was taken to the Metropolitan State Hospital for psychiatric evaluation.

BOTH DRIVERS in a two-car crash at Ronda, Spain, in March 1994, were found to be completely naked when cut from their vehicles. A policeman remarked: "One guy said the collision stripped him. But we don't believe him."

AN ISRAELI COURT ordered a girl of 16 to stop walking around her home naked, in September 1983. Her grandfather, 80, complained that she was trying to give him a heart attack, so that she could inherit his fortune.

Maria Catena, 24, had something slightly similar in mind in 1992 when she stripped naked in front of her bank manager: she was trying to persuade him to give her a loan. He called the police instead, and she ended up with a 16-month suspended sentence for extortion.

ANGRY PREACHER Peter Fransen became so fed up with the constant chattering in his congregation at El Paso, Texas, in 1994, that he stopped his sermon, dropped his trousers and mooned at them. He was later sacked.

TWO SLEEPY HAMPSHIRE VILLAGES were the scene of three appearances within an hour by a blonde flasher who only exposed herself to other women, in January 1988.

Described by the police as being aged 20 to 25 and with "a smart businesswomanlike appearance" she was, in fact, wearing only high heels and a beige raincoat. She began by showing everything to two separate teenage girls in Fleet, then half an hour later she was in Hartley Wintney, where she opened the coat to a 30-year-old woman.

Another female flasher had different targets in 1989. Described as a "buxom beauty" in her forties, she tricked her way into the homes of several solitary old men in Burnham, Bucks, by asking if she could wait there for a neighbour. Once inside, she removed her only garment, a red coat. One of her pensioner victims had collapsed with shock.

IN WHAT SOUNDS like a highly dubious piece of reporting from October 1994, we're told that a flasher in Bonn, Germany, won't be doing it again: his victim's Alsatian bit his penis off.

CHAPTER SEVEN

Out Of Control
Birth Control

Contraception might seem a remarkably simple subject to most people, but then it's often the simplest things that can make life most complicated...

PRESUMABLY PREPARING for a heavy date, seven well-dressed gentlemen carrying automatic weapons broke into a warehouse in Bogota, Colombia, in January 1992. Then they locked the staff in the bathroom and made off with half a million condoms.

FAMILY PLANNERS hit a snag in 1973 when they tried to teach Aboriginal women in South Australia a song giving advice on contraception. The women thought all they had to do to avoid pregnancy was sing the song. There seemed to be little improvement in the situation by 1988, when health advisers found Aborigines reluctant to take advice about condoms, because the spoken word sounded too similar to *quandong*, a fruit tree. They changed the name to "frenchies".

TWO MONTHS after an unnamed Swedish couple watched a performance by metal-bender Uri Geller in 1974, the woman went to her doctor, who confirmed she was pregnant. This was somewhat puzzling, as the woman had had several trouble-free years using IUD contraception. The doctor discovered that her copper coil was so bent out of shape as to be no longer any use. The reluctant parents-to-be surmised it was the result of watching Geller doing his tricks with spoons.

ACCORDING TO Omar Tufan, a senior health official quoted in the Turkish daily newspapers in 1990: "The main reason family planning has failed in south-eastern Turkey is the propaganda carried out by the Kurdish Workers Party". The Kurdish rebels had been telling women that intra-uterine coils were spying devices. Exactly what the information reported would be is far from clear.

JENNIFER AND DAN Skadeland decided to call it quits after the difficult, premature birth of their third child. Dan had a vasectomy, which is allegedly 99.9% effective. Nonetheless, a fourth child turned up, so Jennifer had a tubal ligation, in which the fallopian tubes are tied to prevent eggs passing into the uterus. Their family doctor said he believed there was a 1-in-4,000 chance of tubal ligation failing. In October 1993 Jennifer gave birth to their fifth child, a baby boy, at Fostoria, Ohio. So much for the odds.

A DUTCHMAN who was about to be married needed a circumcision, and went into hospital in 1992 to get it "done by professionals". When he woke up, the prospective bridegroom found that, because of a mix-up in patient cards, he had been given a vasectomy by mistake.

NAVAL HISTORIAN Peer Kluewer managed to solve the mystery of 2,000 condoms found aboard the sunken Nazi submarine U534 in August 1992, working out at 40 condoms per crew member. Visions of gay subsurface orgies disappeared when he realised that they were to be blown up and left to float on the surface to confuse enemy radar.

LEROY GRANT had a bit of explaining to do at Marylebone magistrate's court in March 1991, when he was charged with stealing £52 worth of condoms. He told the court that he used them to waterproof plant pots.

IN BRISBANE, Australia, Damien Russell Stuart, 18, was fined A$85 for wilfully damaging a police car with a condom. Originally arrested for obstructing police and punching a tow truck, Stuart unwrapped a condom as he was being driven to the police station and put it on the floor of the car, where the lubricant caused a circular stain. One could be forgiven for thinking that the cops had decided to throw the book at the guy, and that this was just another item on the list...

ITALIAN PHYSICS STUDENT Lino Missio, 26, was granted a patent in 1994 for his musical condom, which plays Beethoven when the sheath splits. It's coated with a special compound that changes its electrical properties when the sheath tears; at the base a minute microchip, flexibly designed to avoid discomfort, detects the change and triggers an alarm. Missio explained that it needn't just play music. It could give a verbal warning instead. He said he had a prototype, and it worked just fine.

AT ZHANGTIAN village, in south China's Jiangxi

province, 63 children became ill after they ate contraceptive pills in mistake for candy. *China Disaster Reduction News* reported the incident in July 1992, saying that two six-year-olds were playing near the village's government office building before school when they found more than 400 pills wrapped in an old newspaper and thrown out of a window.

IN THE NORTHERN PHILIPPINES province of Bontoc, the birth rate is rising so rapidly that president Fidel Ramos made a special announcement while celebrating his 66th birthday there in March 1994. The Philippines already has a population of 65 million, growing at more than three per cent a year, but, as the country is predominantly Catholic, Ramos could hardly recommend contraception. Instead he decided to hand over 3 million pesos to set up a cable-television connection "in order for you to do something else in the evening, in the hours of darkness".

Marriages Made in Heaven (and Hell)

**"Marry in haste, repent at leisure".
Well, maybe. From serial bigamy to literal
slavery, there are some pretty odd
marriages around...**

A LOS ANGELES BUSINESSMAN, identified only as
Arnold G., proposed to his girlfriend Carol in 1984 and
asked her parents for their consent. After the engagement had
been announced, Carol's father took Arnold aside and told
him his daughter was born by artificial insemination because
he was unlikely to father a child. He named the sperm bank,
which turned out to be one that Arnold had donated to as a
student. Arnold obtained a court injunction to inspect the
records and found that he was the father of his bride-to-be,
and 806 other children. The wedding was called off.

MOZAMBIQUE CHIEFTAIN Zeze Ogoun, from the village of Iksa, was reported in 1990 as having 365 wives, one
for every night of the year. He was then 43, having married

all 365 wives at once when he was 25. Villagers were said to remember the roar when all his wives said "I do" at once. Some 1,800 children resulted from Zeze's visits to a different wife each night, and Zeze was starting to complain of exhaustion and depression: his eldest sons were beginning to covet his youngest wives, while he occasionally had to drive off attention-seeking youngsters with a whip. Many younger warriors apparently hoped to take his place, but he had a few words of warning for them: "The children are unruly and many of the wives smell like goats."

ONE WONDERS why it took so long for anyone to notice, but in September 1990 an unnamed 27-year-old man from Sichuan Province, China, was executed for selling into slavery his wife, mother, daughter and 18 other women. His slave-trading career began in 1985, and after managing to sell virtually all the women in his neighbourhood, he decided to sell his own family as well.

FIVE MANGYAN TRIBESWOMEN from the Philippines jumped to their deaths from a 700 foot cliff in March 1984, rather than go through with marriages arranged for them with men of a different tribe.

IN INDONESIA, a 41-year-old medicine seller was imprisoned for five-and-a-half months in 1981, for marrying a girl less than 15 years old. When he was released his young wife was waiting to meet him at the prison gate, as were his 14 other wives.

AN INDIAN VERSION of Romeo and Juliet was played out in the state of Andra Pradesh in 1993. A village astrologer told Subba Rao, 20, and his bride Nagalakshmi,

18, that although they were married they'd have to wait more than six months, until the stars were auspicious, before they could have sex. With a month to go, the overheated Rao feigned suicide by smearing granules of pesticide on his lips, in order to make his bride's family relent and allow them to make love. He was dragged off to the nearest clinic in Sattupalli, six miles away, and was discharged in perfect health the same evening.

Believing her husband was dying, Nagalakshmi swallowed the remaining pesticide and her family rushed her to the Sattupalli clinic as her husband was returning by bus. By the time they arrived, the doctor in charge had left, to attend a wedding. This time the pesticide proved fatal, so maybe the astrologer had the right idea after all.

JOSE MEZQUITA was baptised an hour before he married, in February 1994, so that the ceremony could be in church. Two hours after the wedding Jose, 76, died of a heart attack while in bed with his 17-year-old bride in Zafra, Spain.

TEK KOR, who lived with his seven wives and 22 children in Nakhon Pathom, Thailand, finally called a family council in 1985. Despite his successful meatball-vending business, Tek Kor had decided that bringing up so many children was straining his financial resources, and persuaded his wives he should have a vasectomy. Even so, the family was still likely to keep growing. A palmist had told Tek Kor that he would have 12 wives, so although he was going to stop having children, he was still going to look for more women to marry until he'd reached the target.

ROGERSVILLE, TENNESSEE, saw the wedding of Hal Warden and Catherine Trent in February 1986. She was 14 and pregnant; he was 15 and marrying for the second time. Warden had been 12 when he married first, his pregnant girlfriend being 15. They divorced when he was 13.

USING DIFFERENT NAMES to disguise his identity, a Sri Lankan man married 20 women. When he was finally arrested for bigamy, it was discovered that he was also engaged to another 20 women as well. A friend who tried to raise bail for him changed his mind when he discovered that a female relative of his was among the duped women.

CON-MAN and serial bigamist Giovanni Vigliotto died of a brain haemorrhage at the age of 61 in prison at Phoenix, Arizona, in February 1991. He had been jailed for 34 years in 1983 after admitting to marrying 105 women, divorcing very few of them, and generally leaving with all their money after only a few weeks. He was said to have had nearly as many aliases as wives, mostly of an exotic European ring, but was finally revealed to be plain Frederick Bertram Jiff of Brooklyn, New York.

ISLAMIC LAW allows a man to have four wives at a time, but even so police in Sumatra thought Ali Nasib Nasution was going a bit far in 1981. The 28-year-old suddenly added seven new wives to his previous collection of 121, all married within seven years and only 93 of them divorced. Nasution got seven years in jail.

Other high-flyers include Pak Awang, an 84-year-old Malaysian witch-doctor specialising in love-charms, who married his 80th wife in 1988; most of his earlier marriages ended in divorce, though some of his wives died. There's also Udaynath Dakhin Ray, a patent medicine salesman from the state of Orissa, India. In his sixties, he married his 90th bride in 1986. She was 15 years old, and he was reported as saying that whenever he feels old, he simply marries another young bride. He also said that he had vowed to marry 100 women before he died after his first wife abandoned him two weeks into their marriage. 57 wives were said to have left or divorced him, 27 had died. Local police didn't bother him, but his 12 sons said they held him in contempt.

SERIAL BIGAMY isn't just restricted to men, though. In 1991, Pat Jackson, 37, was ringing up her tenth marriage, several of which had been bigamous. She had a penchant for men in uniforms. And in the same year, Linda Essex Chandler, 51, said to be the world's most (legally) married woman, was looking for a divorce to get out of marriage number 22.

LEBAI OMAR of Malaysia was arrested with his lover Doyah Dan in 1977 when they were found to be living together outside wedlock. He was put on probation, while she, being unable to pay her fine, was jailed for two months. Omar cycled 17 miles to pay her fine, free her, take her home and marry her. His 40-year-old bride was his 18th wife, the previous 17 unions having ended in divorce; Omar himself was 117.

THERE WAS UPROAR in Fatehabad, Bangladesh, when a 104-year-old priest married a girl of 16... not because of the age gap, but because she was his fifth wife, thus breaking the Islamic limit of four. Villagers wanted him expelled from the priesthood; he said he was marrying the girl, an orphan, to save her from starvation.

At the opposite end of the spectrum, 14-year-old Suldano, from Kenya, revealed a rather limited vision of marital joy when she explained why she was marrying 100-year-old Muhammad Aloo in 1984: "Older men really know how to treat a girl," she said. "He is always kind and never beats me."

AUTHORITIES IN ODESSA, TEXAS, decided not to prosecute a 91-year-old woman in January 1994 after she fatally struck her 91-year-old husband of 67 years with a cane. She explained that he had become too boisterous in demanding sex.

By contrast, a 73-year-old husband from Hampshire called the police in 1986 when his wife, who was the same age, kept demanding sex with him. He feared his heart would not take the strain.

TO COMBAT a drought, farmers in Rangpur province in Bangladesh caught frogs and married them to each other to encourage rain, in May 1995. Both Islamic and Hindu wedding ceremonies were used, and the hitched frogs were then released back into the ponds where they were caught. "I've done it before and it worked," one farmer said, after at least 12 frog weddings had taken place in a few days.

CHAPTER NINE

Bonkers

Carry on copulating seems to be the watchword, regardless of time, place or what the neighbours might think...

A SWEDISH TAXI DRIVER was jailed in October 1994 for leaving the meter running while he had sex with a woman customer and billing her for £5,600. The 34-year-old driver said the bill included 25 occasions of "sexual coitus", charges for trips, hotel and telephone costs, as well as a 25 per cent sales tax. The court decided that he was exploiting the 49-year-old woman, convicted him of usury, sentenced him to three years' jail, and ordered him to pay her back.

THE WEATHER WAS HOT AND HUMID on the May bank holiday in 1992, when John Henderson, 29, and Zoë D'Arcy, 19, who worked together in the Sainsbury's warehouse in West Ealing, London, were returning by train from a day trip to Margate. D'Arcy was seen performing fellatio in a first class compartment by a woman who boarded at

Whitstable with her children. The couple then moved to a packed second class carriage. D'Arcy went to the lavatory, returned carrying her jeans, and sat on Henderson's lap.

The two performed "full sexual intercourse". None of the other passengers in the compartment made any comment, until the couple lit cigarettes afterwards, in a no-smoking carriage. This serious breach of etiquette prompted a furious row, followed by a complaint to the guard. Henderson and D'Arcy were fined £50 each with £25 costs.

A SCHOOLBOY and girl, both 16, had sex in a classroom in front of at least a dozen students at Chattanooga High School in June 1988. They were arrested and charged with agreeing to perform a sex act for money.

NOT PERFORMING for anything was an Israeli school-teacher in 1979, who stopped making love to his wife because he "got fed up". When he hadn't slept with her for more than a year, she complained to a rabbinical court which declared him a "rebellious husband". The court ordered him to have sexual relations with his wife, or pay a weekly fine of 36 pieces of gold until he did so.

A FOOTBALL FAN in the Czech Republic was jailed after he forced his wife to have sex with his favourite team's striker. The fan hoped it would help him score more goals.

NO SUCH COMPULSION was necessary for Ute Winter, 29, wife of a football club president in Mainz, Germany: she slept with the whole of the first team, all the reserves, and had started into the over-40s old-boys eleven, bringing her score up to 28, all footballers, by the end of the 1985 season. Her husband Klaus was obsessed with the club, raising funds for a new clubhouse and personally mixing cement for it at the weekends, leaving blonde Ute to her own devices. The first sign of trouble came when Klaus arrived home and discovered Ute in bed with his star striker. He decided to forgive his wife to avoid a scandal, but later found her with the outside-left in a back room at the clubhouse; the goal-keeper in a car; and the inside-right in his own living room. Klaus decided that was enough, at which point friends finally told him Ute's full-time score. He was granted a divorce.

A SPECTATOR SPORT of a different kind was provided by a couple who made love in their room at the SkyDome Hotel in Toronto in May 1990. The hotel is built inside the Toronto Blue Jay's baseball stadium, with 70 rooms giving a direct view of the playing field. The rooms, of course, can also be directly viewed by the stadium spectators, which meant that when the Blue Jays played the Seattle Mariners, not everyone's attention was on the game.

NEIGHBOURS CALLED THE POLICE when they heard blood-curdling screams in Reading, Berkshire, in May 1994. Officers burst into the house, only to find the row emanating from a deaf couple making love. The pair, in their thirties, had switched off their hearing aids and had no idea how much noise they were making.

A WOMAN who had three-in-a-bed sex with identical twins won a court battle to prove her son's 'uncle' was actually his father, in June 1994. Scientists were said to be baffled because of the genetic similarities, but the court in Celle, Germany, ruled that her husband's twin brother was the father of the four-year-old boy, and so should pay maintenance for him.

THE EARTH MOVED for Darryl Washington, 32, and Maria Ramos, 30, as they got into a passionate clinch – but it was the rumble of an underground train. In September 1992, the couple put a mattress down over the tracks in what they thought was a disused tunnel under Manhattan, New York. It wasn't. Train driver Jose Arrigia slammed on the breaks when he saw them, and Maria frantically tried to get Darryl out of the way; but he thought she was just being more passionate. She escaped with cuts and bruises; he suffered a broken leg and fractured vertebrae.

ADMITTING that some had called her a bimbo, slut or whore, Annabel Chong, 22, told reporters as she arrived in Los Angeles in January 1995 for her latest world record attempt that she simply enjoyed her body. The Singapore-born sociology student and porn actress was attempting to set a new record by having intercourse with 300 men in 10 hours. She said that her advert for volunteers had brought 12,700 replies from around the world, especially from Sweden and Germany. The chosen 300 were told to bring an Aids certificate and a condom. Ms Chong said she had allotted 90 seconds for each man to perform, and had arranged for five women to act as warm-ups. She also said she would be taking a break every two hours to fix her make-up.

Only In It
for the Money

There are some who get it for free, and
some who end up paying for their pleasure.
But once money starts changing hands, all
kinds of curious things can ensue...

SYRIAN-BORN Antoine Moussali complained to the boss of
a lonely-hearts agency in Brussels in June 1987 that he was
only introduced to ugly women. He told Alain Carlier he
wanted to meet a pretty blonde in her twenties, not a lot of
middle-aged widows, one of whom had run up a £110 bill on
champagne. When he said he wanted his £80 fee back, Carlier
attacked him with a knife. As Moussali fled from the office,
Carlier picked up an M-1 rifle and shot him twice in the back.
Moussali died in the street.

ANOTHER DISSATISFIED CUSTOMER was the one at a
Zimbabwean brothel in Bulawayo who blew the place up with
sticks of TNT in February 1990, killing a 15-year-old girl and
demolishing half the building's 64 rooms. Police said the man,

probably a soldier, was aggrieved at the treatment he received from one of the house's 200 girls, who had a notorious reputation for seriously mistreating their clients, although none were ever actually killed. Some customers were said to have been thrown out of windows or "tortured by groups of crazed prostitutes with red-hot irons".

ALMOST AS DISGUSTED was dentist Jacob Beisvitz of Tel Aviv, Israel. In November 1989 Beisvitz rang a call-girl agency because he was feeling lonely after his wife Rachel, 27, had an affair with a neighbour. When the young lady turned up to meet Jacob at a hotel, it turned out to be Rachel, who beat a hasty retreat. The couple next saw each other in the divorce court.

A similar tale emerged from Italy in 1990. Franco Stella, a 35-year-old lorry driver, was given the address of an exclusive brothel in Teramo by a friend. The friend particularly recommended one of the hookers working there. This woman turned out to be Anna, Franco's wife, who had been turning tricks by night without his knowledge. She tried to run away, but he caught her and beat her; she filed charges against him.

FOR TOTAL EMBARRASSMENT, though, one can well imagine the faces of Vatican officials in February 1988, when it was revealed that nuns had been caught up in a VIP prostitution ring in Rome. When detectives uncovered the racket, which was grossing £500,000 a day, they found that many of the girls on offer were either nuns or aristocrats, entertaining politicians and businessmen at leading hotels within a mile or two of the Vatican. One of the group's madames told an investigating magistrate: "If a client wants a nun, we have so many on our books he could even choose which order he would like her to belong to... Carmelite, Benedictine or whatever."

GOING BACK to 1928, we have the tale of Madame Blot, from Rouen, and her 21-year-old daughter. Mlle Blot wished to go to Paris and lead an "immoral life", and told her mother that she was old enough to decide for herself what she should do. Rather than let her daughter be "ruined", Mme Blot got a revolver and shot her dead. She was acquitted of murder.

Times had rather changed by September 1992, when a man from Kuala Lumpur, Malaysia, incensed that his teenage daughter refused to become a prostitute, cut off her hand.

IN AMSTERDAM, the Prostitution Info Centre runs a course of six afternoon lessons, giving a training programme for working girls. Health, techniques and prices are all discussed, along with handling tax-accounts. Condoms, creams, leather wear, whips, false fingernails and the like can all be claimed as tax-deductible expenses in Holland.

Such expenses can tot up, as a survey has revealed that the average Dutchman spends £100 a year on sex. In Holland, the sex industry generates £700 million a year, with prostitutes taking half. Phone sex lines and erotic shows account for most of the rest.

In Norway, though, it's possible to do even more than claim expenses: prostitutes don't have to pay tax at all if they sell their body as a hobby.

TWO TAIWANESE grandmothers, both 78, were arrested for prostitution in August 1993. They told police they became street-walkers because they could not resist their sexual urges.

Police raiding a brothel in Montevarchi, Italy, in 1991, found the madame sitting in her salon furnished with antiques and old lace. She was the white-haired Countess Wanda Venturi von Rutschmann, aged 90.

ANOTHER SPRIGHTLY OLDSTER was Agnes Cowan, 66, of London, Ontario, arrested in 1989. Besides supplementing her old age pension by running a "sexual services consulting company", of which she was the only employee, she also campaigned in the local elections for her own Space Beings and UFOs party.

AT THE OTHER END of the scale, a child prostitution ring was broken up by police in Brattleboro, Vermont, in September 1983. No adults were involved, except as customers, and the operation was run entirely by the ten boys and girls involved, aged between eight and thirteen. No charges were brought because of their ages.

A WOMAN accused of prostitution who said she had had intercourse with 2,000 men as the high priestess of an 'ancient' sex-worshipping church in Los Angeles was sentenced in December 1989 to 360 days' jail for breaking her probation order.

TWO JOURNALISTS, we're told, booked into a Luxembourg hotel which seemed more horrible than usual, with murky bedrooms, shared bathrooms and the impression that the hotel was related to the whorehouse next door. Eventually they went down to the desk and asked outright: "Are you connected to the brothel next door?" "Certainly not," the receptionist replied. "This is an entirely separate brothel."

Doctor, Doctor!

**If anyone ought to be well-adjusted about sex, you'd think it would be the medical profession, dealing as they do with the human body every day.
How wrong one can be...**

AN OPTICIAN appeared in court at Brasschaat, Belgium, in March 1995, and his lawyer Henri Janssens admitted that the charge was technically true: before prescribing contact lenses, his client did frequently ask women to strip naked and dance around his consulting room while he played the accordion. However, Janssens claimed that there were mitigating circumstances: his client had qualified in England where, he assured him, such techniques were commonplace. The optician was later acquitted.

THERE MUST be something about eye specialists: in Monticello, Iowa, optometrist Gary Fisher claimed to have "legitimate medical reasons" for making women shed their blouses during examinations. He said he was simply checking for spine curvatures related to eye problems. The director of the Iowa state physicians board disagreed, and threatened to take him to court in October 1989.

THERE WAS NO LEGITIMATE medical reason whatsoever for the conduct of Michael Whalen, 31, in April 1982. He posed as a doctor from a local hospital in New Orleans, pretending to be part of a fictitious federal programme to teach the elderly how to burp properly. He was charged with fondling the breasts of two women to see if they were qualified as volunteer instructors. He told them that to qualify they had to submit to a breast examination to see whether they burped properly themselves.

TEXAS GYNAECOLOGIST Dr William Michael Clark offered a woman $2,500 to take part in a bogus pain-research project in 1987, "wherein he would spank her and take her blood pressure". He spanked her okay, but welshed on the money. Clark lost his licence, but not his supporters: they said he was the only doctor they knew who'd do housecalls.

IN LOUISIANA, a surgeon was ordered to pay a nurse £3,000 in March 1994 for shooting her in the bottom with a surgical staple while she bent over in the operating theatre.

DURING A PHYSICAL CHECK-UP in November 1991, Dr D'Avis of Illinois asked his patient whether he should check for haemorrhoids. Consent was given, but during the rectal examination, d'Avis asked if the patient was enjoying it. The patient then turned round and saw that, while performing the examination with one hand, the doctor was masturbating with the other. The case came to court, where the judge found d'Avis guilty of assault, and sentenced him to one year's probation.

CHINESE ACUPUNCTURIST Bernard Lee from Reading, Berkshire, was accused of fondling his assistant's breasts in 1989. He claimed he was searching between Melanie Longmore's breasts for an acupuncture point called the 'jing jong'. Miss Longmore, who was dismissed, claimed she was the victim of sexual discrimination.

IN RILIEVO, a small town near Trapani in Sicily, an unemployed plumber by the name of Antonio Sugameli decided to take up faith-healing in 1982. He was 41, with a wife and ten children to support, and the money started to roll in: in his second year of practice he took £30,000. Cures were daily occurrences and his fame spread. It was only in 1984 that people started to notice how many young women were involved.

It seems that in order to transmit his healing powers, Sugameli had to seduce women: even if it were a grandfather or uncle who was ill, a young female member of the family seemed to be the only one who could receive his transmitted powers. One woman went back to him 32 times, to cure her aunt of sciatica. Sugameli had convinced her that she had to make the sacrifice on her aunt's behalf. Eventually, though, Sugameli seduced a newly-married woman who came to him seeking a cure for her father's arthritis. She immediately told her husband, and word spread among the town's male population. It seemed that Sugameli had made love to half the town's young women, many of whom went back to him regularly; at least two women went to his office every day. When the news finally broke, the town's men besieged Sugameli's house, and he had to phone the police and ask them to take him into protective custody. They charged him with fraud and deception, but as Sugameli pointed out: "I never had any complaints. They even paid me for the cures."

UPPER-CRUST BRITISH DOCTOR Rodney Wood, 60, was a pillar of society in Southampton, Long Island. Yet he and his 44-year-old wife Nancy were arrested in Eugene, Oregon, in 1989, after handing out leaflets to male students at the University of Oregon. The leaflets asked for young men between 18 and 23 to participate in a scientific experiment to determine the "sexual potential of the mature female". Each participant would be paid £6 to help show the female's response "to intercourse with one or more males". As it happened, the "mature female" in question was Nancy Wood. They were each fined for attempting to lure students into a sex-trap.

ARTIFICIAL INSEMINATION expert Dr Cecil Jacobson, 55, was found guilty in March 1992 of using his own sperm to make women pregnant, rather than sperm from anonymous donors, as he'd claimed. Dubbed "the Sperminator" by the press, Jacobson was believed to have fathered 75 children at £5,000 a time. He also tricked women at his clinic in Alexandria, Virginia, into believing they were pregnant when they weren't. He was convicted on 52 counts, and faced a fine of £300,000, along with jail sentences totalling 280 years.

Phone-ication

You may think you know what phone sex is all about, but these tales of the telephone shed new light on the idea of electric sex-aids...

PAT LEIGH WAS WOKEN in the early hours at home in Marden, Wiltshire, by two phone calls, in July 1994. On the first occasion she heard groaning and moaning and assumed it was an obscene call. When the phone rang again, she heard more groaning and her daughter Amanda, 25, cry: "Oh my God!" Then she heard a man's voice. Thinking her daughter was being attacked, she rang the police who rushed to Amanda's home in Wokingham, Berkshire. There they found that Amanda had been enjoying a night of passion with her boyfriend. It was assumed that one of them had twice unwittingly pressed the last-number redial button on the bedside phone with a toe.

AN UNNAMED BOY of 16 from Olpe, near Cologne in Germany, decided to ring up a sex line while his parents were on holiday in July 1992. The number he chose was in

Australia, and as the woman went through her husky moaning and groaning, the boy grew so bored he fell asleep. He woke up seven hours later to find her still panting away, and in the meantime he'd run up a phone bill of £750. He was forced to take a summer job to repay his parents.

UNEMPLOYED Raymond Pickess, 40, spent most of his money making 9,000 obscene phone calls: he made about 150 a day in London and the surrounding counties. He dialled numbers at random, and told women who answered that he was going to rape their daughters in his car. When charged with making threatening and obscene calls in 1982, his defence counsel blamed the activities on the fact that he was brought up under the influence of the strict Christian Brethren sect.

A LOVESICK STUDENT in Austria upped the total to 10,000 harassing phone calls to Harvard University students, at a cost of $30,000. He would dial the university prefix number and then continue at random, threatening to kill any women who answered. Calling more than 10 Harvard students a day in a three year period up to 1992, he sometimes called the same student 50 times a day. He had once been spurned by a Harvard student.

The record-holder in our files, though, is Leo Kazan, a 27-year-old assistant editor at a small New York publishing company. In November 1984 he was nabbed for making 13,000 obscene phone calls: his targets were mainly students at Yale.

POSING AS A HEALTH OFFICIAL investigating complaints of theft among cleaning staff at an Eastbourne nursing home in 1989, 50-year-old chartered accountant David Cherry spent three hours talking to a nursing sister. During this time he persuaded her to carry out an intimate body-search of a young woman cleaner, searching inside her jumper and feeling her breasts, taking down her trousers and checking between her legs, and hacking off three inches of her hair. Police were called when the cleaner collapsed in tears. The call was traced to Cherry's home in Harlow, Essex. He admitted having made thousands of similar calls, and to having a fixation about hair because a nurse once cut his while treating a head injury. Despite his distance from the scene, Cherry was charged with assaulting the cleaner.

A PHONE HOAXER in Fort Lauderdale, Florida, called at least 125 women in 1983. He claimed to be holding hostage a relative, and would harm them if the woman didn't comply with his demands. These included going out naked in the street and, in one case where his demands were complied with, making love with a complete stranger while the hoax-er listened over the phone.

KENNETH COHEN, 47, vice-president of the Metro-media Corporation in New York, specialised in phoning up women and pretending to be their husband's sex therapist. He told them that their husbands were on the verge of suicide and that their lives could only be saved by satisfying their sexual fantasies. One woman seduced her next-door neighbour, who was innocently mowing the grass, and then proudly told her husband when he came home that she had done exactly what the therapist had ordered. Only then did her husband tell her that he didn't have a sex therapist. Cohen was arrested in August 1984.

MOST EXTRAORDINARY of the phone hoaxers is "Dr Bender" from Cologne in Germany. His real name was

Manfred Kah, a 29-year-old bank manager. He made more than 1,000 phone calls to all parts of the country, always following the same routine. He would tell women that he had a relative of theirs in his casualty ward with a malignant disease. It would therefore need a special consultation to test them for the virus. One woman explained that she had agreed to meet the doctor in a hotel room, and he had said that the examination would be painless, but rather embarrassing to him. He suggested she wear a blindfold "to keep matters impersonal and medical", and that she must have an orgasm for him to be certain if she had the virus or not. He then made love to her three times "to make sure of the diagnosis". Later he told her that the test was negative, and advised her to take two aspirins at night for a week.

Other women sat waiting for him, blindfolded, in their cars; one woman was told to bring a rug so he could examine her in the woods. It seems Kah made love to at least 162 women, before a student, who'd arranged to meet him in a hotel, became suspicious. She told the police and a woman detective took her place. When Kah had stripped for action, a male detective leapt out of the wardrobe and arrested him.

RAYMOND MITCHELL III, of Nashville, Tennessee, pulled a similar stunt in 1995. He would phone up his victims late at night and, in a sexy whisper, persuade them to unlock their doors, undress, put on a blindfold and wait for him in bed. At least three women did so, thinking he was their boyfriend, and had sex with the so-called Fantasy Man – one woman twice a week for two months. She only realised the truth when the blindfold slipped. Mitchell, 45, was charged with rape-by-fraud.

Beastly Tales

"Never work with animals" goes the old actors' saying. Never have sex with them either, unless you want to end up in court. Yet sometimes, it seems, they want to have sex with us. Both types of tales are represented in the following selection...

PAUL GRIPTON and his family got a quite a surprise when they visited the West Midlands Safari Park at Bewdley, Worcestershire, in February 1995. Having driven from his home in Wednesfield, Wolverhampton, Paul was sitting there with his wife and two sons in their Ford Fiesta, waiting for a queue of traffic to get moving, when they were approached by Christopher, a 12-foot-tall giraffe weighing half a ton. Christopher had decided to try to mate with their car, straddling it and rocking back and forth while the roof slowly crumpled and the bonnet caved in. The good news was that the randy giraffe gave up after about a minute and moved off, by which time the bodywork was so buckled that Paul had to kick open the doors before the terrified family could get out. The bad news was that his insurance policy did not cover damage caused by frustrated giraffes.

A RANDY ELK charged Kari Hauge, 33, as she went cross-country skiing in Norway, in January 1995. The elk was six feet tall at the shoulder and obviously aroused, and Kari knew she couldn't escape. She stood her ground and then, as the elk closed in, used a trick learned in self-defence classes. She stuck her fingers in its nostrils. As the elk collapsed with shock, she made her getaway.

MICHAEL HALE, 19, was windsurfing in a wet-suit near his home at Walton-on-the-Naze in Essex at the beginning of 1991. He was attacked by a frisky 30-stone bull seal, which mistook him for a mate and tried to get on board. Hale hit the water in an attempt to scare it off, but that only made it roar with excitement. The courtship lasted 90 minutes before Hale could get ashore.

WOMEN WERE PURSUED by a "love-sick ape" through the main street of Sonepat in the north Indian state of Haryana in November 1986. It sank its teeth into at least two dozen women, and attempts by police to capture the animal failed miserably. Local people believed the ape to be the reincarnation of a frustrated lover.

Nurses at the government-run Sir Maharaja Ghulab Singh hospital in Jammu, Kashmir, had rather different ideas about Romeo the rude rhesus monkey. To them, he was just a pest. He'd molested 30 young women, groping at their breasts and trying to kiss and cuddle them. Although staff threw stones at him, he was undeterred. Nurses threatened to strike when he began making obscene gestures. In 1992 he was finally trapped by police and wildlife officials, and, after 66 days behind bars, banished to the jungle.

DEBORAH CLARKE, 26, was angry when her husband Winston, 41, told her his company was moving from St Louis, Missouri to San Francisco. All her family and friends were in St Louis, but as Winston was a senior executive, they had to move. They had no children, and, as Winston was still going to have to make frequent trips back to St Louis, he made a concession, telling his wife she could have a pet — even though he hated animals. The slim brunette chose a cockatoo, and set about teaching him how to talk. Soon he could say "Deborah", "I'm hungry", "feed me" and "goodbye".

The phrase the bird seemed to like most, however, was "Hi, y'all", a common expression in the American South. In September 1982, Winston arrived at the apartment block and was greeted by 23-year-old doorman Jimmy Joe Bromley with a smiling "Hi, y'all". A week later, Winston snapped. Driving home in his new Cadillac, he spotted Bromley at the building's entrance, and rammed his car through the doors. Bromley dodged, escaping with cuts and scratches, but the car was wrecked and £8,000 worth of damage was done to the foyer. The cockatoo told no lies: Deborah had indeed been having an affair with Bromley. Not that the knowledge did Winston much good: she sued for divorce on the grounds that he'd deserted her for his job, and the building owners sued for damage to the foyer.

WEDDING GUESTS got something of a surprise when they sat down to watch a video of the reception in Sussex in 1994. The man shooting the reception pictures had borrowed the video camera from Derek Jeffrey, 59, who had forgotten to erase the footage on the tape, and thus presented the guests with a pornographic 10-minute movie of himself committing acts of bestiality with his neighbour's dog. Jeffrey was seen lying on a bed, naked but for his socks, with a Staffordshire bull terrier called Ronnie.

Brought to court, Jeffrey said that he made the film after he and three friends had watched a video called *Animal Farm* showing women having sex with animals. Besides admitting to being drunk at the time, he said that he made the video to prove such pornographic movies used trick photography, and that no sex had actually taken place with the dog. The jury failed to believe him, and he received a six-month suspended sentence.

POLICE IN TUCSON, ARIZONA, arrested a 41-year-old man in September 1994 who appeared to be trying to coax horses from the University of Arizona Agriculture Center toward him with food, which he was holding near his exposed penis as if to invite oral sex. The police had warned the man about similar behaviour three months before.

IN KENYA, Peter Wambugu Mugo proclaimed in court: "You accuse me of wickedness, but if I'd killed the sheep and sold it to the butcher, you'd all have queued up to buy a bit." Rather than killing the sheep, he was actually charged with abducting it and having carnal knowledge of it. The owner of four sheep, noticing one missing, went looking for it and found it in a nearby copse. It was tethered to a bush, and Mugo was standing behind it, naked, singing a lullaby and thrusting in time to the music. He was overpowered by furious members of the public when the alarm was raised.

In court in 1993, he explained that he had sex with the animal because he was no longer able to afford VD treatment. "Five times I go with women, five times I get VD," he said.

He also pleaded not guilty to urinating in an ashtray at Barclay's Bank, Voi Town, claiming he had a weak bladder and was being held prisoner by the bank manager at the time. He was found guilty on all counts and imprisoned for two years.

EQUALLY ABSURD is the tale from Zimbabwe of the unnamed man who had sex with a cow because he was afraid of catching Aids from a human partner. On his court appearance in March 1995, he declared that he was in love with the cow, recited marriage vows from the dock, and promised to be faithful to the animal while serving his sentence in jail. He got nine months.

A MOROCCAN MAN was charged in 1981 with sexually assaulting a pelican on the Greek island of Syros. The pelican was the mascot of the neighbouring island of Tinos, and enraged islanders attacked Abdel Brim Talal after the dying bird was found in a public toilet. The pelican, a male, had been sexually assaulted, and Talal was found with blood and feathers on his clothes. In what may seem an entirely inappropriate method of preservation, the bird was later stuffed.

A MOST BIZARRE CASE is that of the man who worked at the San Antonio Zoo in Texas in 1984 and 1985. The 27-year-old was caught by postal inspectors when he mailed photos to *Hustler* magazine, and finally confessed to having sex with cats, dogs, horses, ponies, goats, sheep, cows, a pig and a duck... and an oryx, a gazelle and a baboon. He was hoping to get a job at Sea World of Texas, so he could also have sex with a dolphin.

LONDON TRANSPORT LABOURER John Smith was charged with the common law offence of "committing an act of a lewd, obscene and disgusting nature and outraging public decency by behaving in an indecent manner with a cat to the great disgust and annoyance of diverse of Her Majesty's subjects within whose purview such an act was committed." The act was committed just before Christmas 1989 on a tube train, after Smith had drunk 10 pints of beer. He said he was dead to the world until people began shouting at him. When arrested, he asked the police "What cat?" He was fined £500, and was thought likely to lose his job because he "could not cope with the constant stream of jokes directed at him."

ANGRY COWBOY Ross Howard of Denver, protesting about men being allowed marry men, was refused a licence to marry his horse in 1992. The hitch was a technicality: Colorado law says that three-year-olds need parental consent.

SABINE GRONAU, 25, of Schwaebische Alb in Southern Germany, was all too eager to respond to an appeal to help save the mountain gorilla species from extinction in 1992. Already having three sons of her own, she offered to have a baby gorilla by artificial insemination. Her husband was rather less keen, though he told her to do what she wanted. A gynaecologist said such a birth would be impossible, as her body would reject the embryo.

ANNE PERKINS, a graduate student at the University of California working on the sexuality of sheep, ran into problems when she tried to extend the study to include the possibility of ewe-on-cwe encounters. She confessed: "It is very difficult to look at the possibility of lesbian sheep because if you are a lesbian sheep, what you do to solicit sex is to stand still. Maybe there is a female sheep out there really wanting another female, but there's just no way for us to know it."

FELINA DE LA CRUZ, a 45-year-old laundrywoman from Cabanatuan in the Philippines, caused something of a sensation when she claimed to have given birth to an 18-centimetre mudfish on 13 October 1990. She called the fish Angeline Dyesebel and tried to bottle-feed it in front of journalists; a gathering crowd insisted, "it's sucking, it's sucking!" Her husband Romeo said he heard the fish say "ik-ik" shortly after his wife delivered it, but admitted there were no witnesses. When large crowds began to damage the de la Cruz home, the fish was transferred to an aquarium at the mayor's house, and given an armed guard. It died a couple of months later, despite regular bottle-feeding. The aptly named Dr Juan Concepcion was convinced, however, that Mrs de la Cruz had never been pregnant in the previous nine months.

MORE GULLIBLE, perhaps, was Nathaniel St Andre, sergeant-surgeon to King George I, who was duped by one Mary Tofts into believing that she had given birth to 17 rabbits in 1726. St Andre was ever-afterwards known as the 'Rabbit Doctor'.

IT SOUNDS like an extremely unlikely tale, even if it does originate in the *British Medical Journal*: in 1992, the 22-year-old owner of an Irish red setter found that his dog had only one testicle. This prompted him to check his own tackle, and he found that he only had one as well. "This is a new twist to the widely held belief that people may resemble their pets," commented the *Journal*.

EXTENSIVE RIOTING PLAGUED Conakry, the capital of Guinea in West Africa, in 1992. It all began with a rumour that Spanish businessman Alseny Gomez was offering young women to have sex with dogs. He narrowly escaped a lynch mob which then ran amok for three days, stoning foreign cars and raping Guinean women dressed in Western-style clothes. Later investigation discovered that the story had been made up by Gomez's nightwatchman to scare off an unwanted girlfriend.

CHAPTER FOURTEEN

Strange Penetrations

Rape and assault are never subjects to be taken lightly, but some of these events have stranger overtones than others...

A WOMAN WHO FAINTED at the mere mention of the word 'sex', took William Gray, 42, to court in Cincinnati in 1993, accusing him of felonious sexual penetration after he whispered the word in her ear in the lobby of her apartment building, causing her to pass out. The unnamed 39-year-old claimed that Gray knew she would faint, assaulted her, then persuaded the apartment building manager to help him carry her to her room, where he assaulted her again.

The woman's reaction was caused by an unusual psychological syndrome called conversion hysteria, which can cause paralysis, voice loss, seizures or fainting in response to a word; or in this case, 26 different words. Apart from 'sex', she also fainted at the mention of 'intercourse', 'copulation', 'breasts', and the coarser items in the sexual vocabulary; but she also fainted at 'adoption', 'anorexia' and, most curious of all, at the name of the singer 'Karen Carpenter'. The woman fainted six times at preliminary hearings, after which it was decided to substitute the word 'nookie' for 'sex'. Gray's lawyers, while not doubting the truth of the woman's condition, were forced to ask how she could recognise her attacker if she was unconscious at the time. For Gray himself, it seems, such questions were irrelevant: he pleaded not guilty by reason of insanity.

SPRING 1993 saw a curious phenomenon in Sweden, where a large number of women reported being knocked out by something in their drinks. Typically, the incidents took place in bars where, after one or two sips of their drinks, they blacked out completely. One woman woke on a park bench where some men tried to abduct her before she was rescued.

After the first press reports, more women came forward, and the phenomenon seemed to spread like wildfire. Several claimed to have been sexually abused as well as drugged, and one middle-aged woman said she had been abducted and "raped for hours" before being thrown out in the street with her clothes torn to shreds. "She was fully aware of what happened, but couldn't lift a finger to prevent it," said a police spokesman, who was convinced all the reports were true. Even so, no one was arrested and the panic died away amid tales that the cause was cheap illegal spirits being imported from Russia, or that someone had slipped LSD into the ladies' beers.

A KOREAN-BORN WAITRESS, known only as 'Sarah', 27, was the victim in a rape trial that came to court in November 1990. She came from Wisconsin, suffered from Multiple Personality Disorder, and had 18 separate personalities, which increased to 46 after the rape attempt. At least one personality seems to have consented to sex, although her dominant personality claimed the man took advantage of her mental illness.

Defendant Mark Peterson, 29, a married supermarket worker, met the woman in a park while she was fishing with friends and manifesting a personality called Franny, a maternal figure aged 30. Two days later, at a restaurant, she introduced him to a number of other personae, including Jennifer, "a fun-loving 20-year-old". Jennifer apparently agreed to have sex with him in her car, saying: "Tell me what sex is and I'll tell you if I enjoyed it." During the intercourse she switched to six-year-old Emily, before returning to Franny, who was horrified to discover what had happened, and phoned the police to report the rape as soon as she got home. After six of Sarah's personalities had testified in the witness box (each taking the oath separately), Peterson was eventually found guilty of raping all but one of her personalities, but was later released on a technicality.

MORE CURIOUS YET is the case of Edward G. Kelly, 44, of Falls Church, Virginia. In 1994, he was charged with raping a woman of 26 he met several months earlier when they were both in group therapy. Both Kelly and the victim claim to suffer from Multiple Personality Disorder. Kelly was accused of tying up the woman with wire and raping her in her home in a Washington suburb. His defence was that one of his personalities, 'Spirit', and one of hers, 'Laura', consented to sex. "There was no forcing, there was no hurting anybody," Kelly said in his deposition to the court. "Spirit loved Laura."

PRISON OFFICER Robin Burnett, 29, received only probation after appearing in court in September 1994 charged with burglary with intent to commit rape and assault.

Burnett, from Sunderland, claimed that he was sleepwalking at the time. He was wearing only his underpants when he forced his way into the house of a 28-year-old woman neighbour at five in the morning and hurled her onto a bed. As she screamed and fought him, he suddenly came to his senses and went home. His defence that he was suffering from insane automatism at the time was accepted by the court.

THE REVEREND Andrew Arbuthnot was allowed to continue his ministry at the London Healing Mission as a freelance, even though his licence to practice as a minister had been withdrawn by the Church of England. It was revealed in December 1994 that part of Arbuthnot's ministry involved the exorcism of women cult-members who had been sexually abused, and included an internal 'cleansing'. An Old Etonian, former merchant banker, Scots Guard and Conservative Party candidate, Arbuthnot is said to have poured wine over his victims' genitals, inserted crucifixes and used his fingers to make the sign of the cross in their vaginas. The Bishop of Wakefield described the practices as "utterly disgusting and blasphemous".

Those Crazy Japanese

Weirdness in sex depends on your point of view. What's normal in one country can seem very strange from a foreign perspective. Even so, the Japanese do seem a little... odd

SCHOOLGIRLS' KNICKERS, worn and unwashed, began selling like hot cakes on the Tokyo sex scene in 1993, at 4,000 yen (£25) a time. Enthusiasts for *Loli-can* (Lolita Complex) get the vacuum-packed white underwear, complete with a photo on the front, supposedly of the item's previous owner, and if they have 11,000 yen, they can get an entire school uniform. One suspects, however, that the price had nothing to do with it when a girl was stopped in the street by men in 1994 and forced to hand over her underwear.

While the main market is for schoolgirls' underwear, six varieties are on offer: junior high, high school, college girl, housewife, nurse and widow. And for those who don't want to go into a sex shop, the knickers are available from the country's ubiquitous vending machines, which sell almost anything.

However, like most things in Japan, where you can do almost anything so long as you do it through the proper channels, there can be problems. In September 1993, three men were arrested for selling used schoolgirl panties from a vending machine in the Tokyo suburbs. Their crime was that they were doing it without an official permit.

Even so, in the same month, the Japanese Education Ministry was ordering a crackdown, telling local prefectural authorities "to use all means to stop the trade". Schoolgirls were said to have been selling their used panties to dealers for about £6 a time.

THE MARKET had moved on by 1994, however. In May, Shukan Isomura of the Wakayama company, which had started the knicker-selling the previous year, announced that he had a new hot seller: fresh schoolgirl's saliva. For 3,000 yen, customers got a 50ml bottle, again with a photo of the donor. Freshness was guaranteed, the saliva being not more than seven days old and kept refrigerated. His Tokyo store was selling 300 units a week. He was also said to be investigating the possibility of selling schoolgirl's menstrual fluid.

NOT TO BE OUTDONE, the Kanebo cosmetics company announced in April 1995 that it had a new line for men wishing to attract women: sweaty underpants. Kanebo have managed to produce synthetic pheromones, found in sweat and known to attract women, and have discovered a way to impregnate fibres with it. A line of sweat-smelling underpants, ties and handkerchiefs is due to go on sale in spring 1996, along with a similar pheromone-laced perfume for men. The only problem is that the smell wears off after about ten washings.

MEN AREN'T THE ONLY TARGETS for this sort of Japanese industriousness, though. In August 1992 it was reported that new vending machines were popping up all over Japan. For 300 yen, women could get a plastic capsule containing a bachelor's name, phone number and details of the type of car he owns.

A BUDDHIST MONK in Osaka knew how to look after his flock. Yoshifumo Ito ran eight 'salons' where pretty young girls offered 'massage' to his faithful male disciples. Ito got three years' jail and a fine of 1.5 million yen.

SAMU YAMAMOTO, a small, none-too-good-looking 42-year-old Tokyo café owner, shot to fame in December 1994 when he published his book, *Diary of Groper*. Groping is precisely what he does, having started at 16 when he accompanied a neighbour to the grocer's. When she bent down to pick up a bunch of radishes, he lunged, and it just went on from there: he claims to have molested many thousands of women since.

"During the height of my groping," he said, "I used to molest perhaps ten women a day. I just bought a train pass and travelled round and round on the circle line... groping."

The groping commuter is legendary on Japan's crowded trains. Yamamoto explains his technique as follows: "First, I have to find a woman to my taste and, next, see if she can be got at and looks quiet. I take advantage of the quiet ones. When you are an expert you can get your hand inside the skirt and sometimes inside her underwear."

He avoids beautiful, confident-looking women who he

expects will retaliate and denounce him, preferring the meek who he calculates won't draw attention to themselves. Often they don't even tell him to stop, but just stand there and allow the groping, after which he moves on to his next target. Sometimes he gets it wrong, and is hauled off for questioning by the police; but so far he's always managed to talk himself out of it. Even so, he's been hit or kicked quite often, and had pins stuck in his hands. Astonishingly, the publication of his book, rather than making him an object of contempt, has turned him into a media star, frequently appearing on TV chat shows.

Even more weirdly, groping is sometimes a group activity as well. Yamamoto and his friends often go to high-school baseball games together, so they can squeeze the cheerleaders. Occasionally, this sort of group grope involves several men standing in a line, thus providing a screen behind which one of their number can feel his victim undetected.

That Obscure Object of Desire

Prepare for a festival of fetishism, from knicker-nickers to sauce-smearers, and body parts from head to toe...

TALES of men stealing women's underwear, usually from washing lines, occur so frequently as to be hardly unusual. Yet there are curious variants...

POLICE SERGEANT Robert Barnes pleaded guilty in 1981 to 60 offences of burglary and theft over 11 years. The City of London policeman's loot consisted entirely of the underwear of women constables. He knew when his victim's houses would be empty because he arranged the duty rosters at Wood Street police station.

IN INDONESIA, a 28-year-old man caught stealing young girls' panties from clothes-lines in 1986 explained that he was not doing it for material gain but to use them in a ritual that would cause him to be "respected and honoured" by other people. He would immerse the stolen panties in a pail or bowl of water, add certain kinds of flowers, then take a bath with the water at prescribed times. He had been stealing panties for the purpose for two years.

FRANK SNEDDON, 34, pleaded guilty to three counts of trying to extort womens' panties in 1980. In one of the cases, occurring in Edmonton, Alberta, a woman returned to her parked car at a shopping centre and found a note and a shotgun shell taped to the windshield. Written in capital letters and without punctuation, the note read: "I SAW YOU GOING INTO THE STORE I LIKE YOUR BODY AND WANT YOUR PANTIES". In the other cases, notes had been left instructing women to leave their panties in phone booths, or to throw them out of car windows.

IN DROGHEDA, Co. Dublin, someone had things the wrong way round in 1988. Instead of stealing knickers from washing lines, he was hanging up new ones, or arranging them in pretty patterns on the lawn.

IN PAINSVILLE, Ohio, Van W. Patterson, 23, added a new twist when he was convicted in 1991 as being the "BVD Bandit", who broke into homes, fondled sleeping men and cut off their underwear. He was found guilty of 21 counts of aggravated burglary, two of robbery and four of sexual imposition, and faced 45 years in jail.

FROM KNICKERS to feet: a young man identified by Los Angeles police only as 'Leonardo Da Toenail' was caught in 1981 after a number of complaints from young women in the library of the University of Southern California that someone had painted their toenails different colours. Posing as a student, Da Toenail would follow his chosen target into the library and sit opposite them apparently engrossed in a project. He would then drop something, duck under the table and surreptitiously daub the object of his desire. Something else would clatter to the floor, and the other big toe would be painted. When arrested he had 16 pots of nail varnish about his person, but charges were dropped when no one wished to testify against him.

RICHARD HUNTER, 21, received a three-month sentence in 1985 for breaking into the New York house of Oyra Ostad to tickle her feet and steal her shoes. He was arrested when he returned three weeks later to do the same to Oyra's elder sister, Farbia.

TOE SUCKING is an all-too-common fetish: among many cases there is the Italian raider who robbed shops in Pisa in 1994 and then forced the girl assistants to let him suck their toes. Dozens of young women were said to have been forced to gratify him. And in St Louis, early in 1992, a jogger was being sought after he had knocked down young schoolgirls on four occasions, sucked their toes and then ran away.

FROM FEET TO SHOES, and another perverted policeman. Charles Hay, 37, of Musselburgh, Scotland, was jailed in 1986 after an eight-year career of assaulting women and stealing their shoes. For the most part he restricted himself to shoe theft, but on one occasion he visited a 22-year-old woman whose husband was in prison, attacked her, tied a pair of tights round her neck, forced her to remove her underwear and put on a pair of boots. Then he bit and licked the boots.

More extreme still was the man in Paris who struck nine times in three months in 1992. Attacking his women victims, he stole their shoes and then forced them to watch, in some bemusement, as he ate their footwear.

WORKING OUR WAY UPWARDS, we come to David Brook of Weymouth, Dorset, whose passion was women's legs. He would writhe on the ground, pretending to be ill, and grab the legs of girls who came to help, smothering their knees with kisses.

AND SO to what must be the fetishist's favourite object: the bottom. Jerome Wright walked into a police station in July 1990 and confessed to being 'Dartman', responsible for at least 55 attacks on women at New York's Pennsylvania Station. The 33-year-old's weapon of assault was a dart made from a large pin, blown through a drinking straw; he targeted the buttocks of well-dressed women in skirts and dresses. Fat women were particularly vulnerable as they made larger targets.

BANBURY IN OXFORDSHIRE was the hunting ground of the 'Phantom Bottom Smacker' in August 1968. Seven girls, all pretty and usually mini-skirted, complained to police, who suspected that many more victims had failed to come forward. Usually operating in his lunch-break, his method was simply to walk up behind his chosen target, administer a sharp slap and run away, often laughing as he did so.

In Sparkhill, Birmingham, an Asian man attacked nine women in autumn 1984, stabbing them in the buttocks with a knife. He wasn't caught, and a year later he was back to strike two more times.

THE ACTIONS OF ARSONIST Terence Goodhew were even more bizarre. In 1988, Goodhew, 32, crept up behind girls on two occasions and set fire to their bottoms as they stood at bus stops in West Ham, London. Having lit their clothing, he then ran away. When arrested, he told police: "I'm careless with matches." His previous convictions included one for stabbing three women in the bottom with a dart. He was jailed for nine months.

TAX COLLECTOR Stephen Davidson, 42, posed as a film producer and, over a six year period up to 1981, spanked thousands of female college students in a phoney search for the perfect screamer. The girls, from Columbia, New York and other universities, were lured to a studio for 'auditions'. Always topless, they were given a red micro-skirt to wear, a straw boater and a Peter Pan collar. Davidson then proceeded to spank them 25 times, and it seems they really believed he was going to offer them a film contract if they screamed well enough. In fact, he and his associates took the opportunity to take tens of thousands of colour photographs of the beatings at the same time, many of which were then sold to girlie magazines and pornography shops.

MADDEST OF ALL was the Illinois Enema Bandit. Between 1965 and 1975, Michael Kenyon, 30 years old at the time of his arrest, forcibly administered enemas to at least two dozen victims, mostly female students. Disguised by a ski mask, he would break into a woman's room, tie her up and get to work with his rubber tubing. He would also steal a single item before leaving his victim trussed up, and would sometimes phone the police to boast about his crime. He began while a student at the University of Illinois, committing a dozen assaults before graduating in 1969. He then made his attacks in various parts of the country, including administering an enema to a girl on a train travelling to

Florida. He returned home in 1974, where on one occasion he attacked several University of Illinois co-eds in a single night. He was finally arrested in connection with two robberies, after which someone noticed that his method of breaking and entering were the same as the Enema Bandit's. He got six years in jail.

IN MALAYSIA, a man was arrested in 1978 after admitting he had stabbed the breasts of more than 20 women with a needle. He was a bra salesman.

AND SO TO HAIR FETISHISTS. In July 1969, a 'Mad Scalper' was causing panic in Dijon, France. Full of Gallic charm, this loony would sit beside pretty girls in secluded places and compliment them on their hair, then ask them for a lock for his collection. If his target refused, he would jump on her, bind and gag her, then whip out his shears and cut off most of her hair.

SECURITY GUARD Keith Everett, 29, gained a reputation as 'Jack the Crimper' in 1985. His thing was to sneak up behind women and girls and rub shampoo or washing-up liquid into their hair for two or three minutes, before running off. He made more than 10 attacks on victims aged between 12 and 34, and got a year's jail for his pains.

THE BEHAVIOUR of Charles O. Guyer, 44, of Bedford, Pennsylvania, was even more bizarre. Rather than ending up in court, he himself was the judge. His mistake was to offer leniency to a 21-year-old man on a drunk and disorderly charge in 1992, if the defendant would let him shampoo his hair. The man submitted to one wash and rinse and was told that he would get more leniency if he persuaded some friends to let Guyer shampoo their hair as well. The man returned with two undercover state troopers, who arrested Guyer; but only after they'd received their shampoos.

FROM PARTS of the body to the whole thing: we start in 1927 with a very high-class case indeed. Sir Gerard Arthur Maxwell Willshire, 36, of Hindhead, went for a drive with 22-year-old Miss Jean Olds, of West Kensington. Stopping in a wood near Maidstone, he ordered Miss Olds to undress, and when she was clad only in her shoes and stockings, he tied her hands behind her and proceeded to cover her naked body with black boot polish. In his defence, he claimed to be suffering from trench fever, caught in the First World War, and to have been drunk, but still got six months for assault. The judge, addressing the jury, expressed the opinion that "refined people" would not wish to listen to the case; but there was a long queue for the public gallery, mostly of women, both young and old.

IN VIRGINIA BEACH, Virginia, an intruder entered a woman's unlocked apartment in 1981 while she was asleep. He then forcibly covered her face and clothed body with chocolate and vanilla cake frosting. He reportedly told his victim that she should have known this would happen if she left her doors unlocked.

A 26-YEAR-OLD office worker was on her way to work in Milwaukee in September 1987. At about 7.20am, she passed an alley on Water Street and saw a man dressed in blue, carrying a garbage bag. She kept walking and he attacked her from behind, pushing her to the ground and pouring wet concrete from the bag all over her. Having emptied the bag, he fled. An arrest was made, but the case never came to court.

"It was weird," said the woman. "I didn't know what to think."

Two bus drivers in Los Angeles didn't know what to think either. Two gunmen boarded their bus in 1982, made the male driver take the wheel and took his woman companion to a back seat. One of the gunmen gave her an unidentified white tablet, telling her: "If you wake up you won't be able to identify us afterwards." Then he stripped her, tied her up, and smothered her naked body in tartar sauce.

RATHER WORSE was Steve Symons, 21, of March, Cambridge. When he saw a girl he fancied, he cut the brake pipes on her car, causing 11 young ladies to have narrow escapes in 1988. He had an obsessive sexual fantasy about women being unable to stop their cars. When arrested, he told police that he was a virgin and didn't have a clue about women. He was also found to have a bag full of bicycle pedal rubbers that he'd stolen.

MOST BIZARRE of all is the case of businessman Matt Simmons, 33, of Anaheim, California. He gets turned on by giving money to women, and has apparently given away £100,000 so far. He has to know the woman for a while, and she can be completely clothed, but if she says "give me your money" he has an orgasm. He went into counselling in 1993, but during one session doctors caught him trying to give $100 to a nurse, after which all female staff were banned.

CHAPTER SEVENTEEN

Coming to a Climax

Normal sex isn't enough for some of us, which is fair enough. But some people have some very odd ways indeed of getting off...

A SHY STUDENT, identified only as 'George', was erotically obsessed with his Austin Metro. The 20-year-old lived at home with his strictly religious parents and had no sexual experience of women at all. He began to fantasize about other Metros he'd seen, but his own was special and photos of it adorned his bedroom. Its front reminded him of a smiling child, and its rear end aroused him. He would seek out quiet places where the two of them could be alone, and then he'd crouch down by its smoking exhaust pipe and masturbate. He was described as "confused but happy". His doctors prescribed a course of "orgasmic reconditioning".

THE WOMEN'S OUTHOUSE in the Montana de Oro State Park, California, was a relatively primitive affair, built over a cesspit at Spooner's Cove. In August 1987, 37-year-old Donald H. Baker from Santa Barbara was arrested by park rangers after he was found sitting waist-deep in the wastepit under the toilet. He had been spotted through a crack in the wall by a man waiting for his wife, and was wearing protective plastic clothing and surgical gloves and sitting on a crate. He had apparently been there since daybreak, with plans to stay all day long. Rangers hosed him off and took him to the County Jail in San Luis Obispo.

RETIRING from the military in 1969 at the age of 49, an unnamed German major found the insecurity of civilian life made him impotent. Eventually he found the answer: when in the mood to make love to his wife, he first found it necessary to march outside and run a flag up the pole outside his house in Cologne. Then he pinned his five WWII medals, including the Iron Cross, Close Combat Bar and Panzer Storm Medal, to his chest. Being naked at the time, the pain did the trick for him, but there was one other problem: he got a skin infection from the medals.

A WOMAN named only as 'Debbi Anne' was arrested in British Columbia, Canada, after a high-speed car chase in 1994. She claimed to be suffering from a "sexual speed fetish", and had been masturbating while at the wheel of her car during the 120mph chase. "I can only come when I smell the aroma of hot tyres," said the 23-year-old blonde, who was ordered to get immediate psychiatric help or face jail. She said she'd be trying to satisfy her desires in future by buying rubber knickers, in the hope that they'd have the same erotic smell.

FIREFIGHTERS were called to a house in Knoxville, Tennessee, in April 1995 when neighbours smelled something burning. There they found the nude body of a 16-year-old boy and called in police. Confronted with posters of heavy-metal rock groups and a cow's heart attached to the boy's genitals, they at first thought they were dealing with a ritual murder. However, they then found several underground pornographic magazines under the boy's bed, one of which, *Ovid Now*, described a 'sex-toy' that could be made from the fresh heart of a cow, a simple electrical circuit and some batteries. The dead heart is made to beat, and then used sexually in a perversion which is apparently gaining popularity in the rural South. The trouble was, the boy had wired up the heart and plugged it into the wall-socket. He died of electrocution, and the electricity had then cooked his remains.

SHOPLIFTER Julie Amri told Chichester Crown Court in 1993 that she could only achieve orgasm by being chased through the streets by police cars or store detectives and being locked in a cell. "It turns me on," she said. "I love the uniforms, the chase and the flashing blue lights." A psychiatrist confirmed she suffered from a disorder which compelled her to steal to gain attention. The 35-year-old divorcee said she had her first orgasm in the back of a police car when she was 28, and found it hard not to think of the association.

A GAY ACTOR received treatment from a sex therapist when he found that the sound of men sneezing turned him on. It was said to be the first known case of a sneezing fetish. The 26-year-old was apparently cured after a series of anti-sneezing sessions in 1990.

DOCTORS X-RAYED Manuela Kleist after a motorbike crash in 1994 and found 60 two-inch needles embedded in her body. The 34-year-old masochist had pushed the needles deep into her breasts, buttocks, thighs, ankles, arms and belly. She told doctors in Monheim, Germany: "I love the pleasures of pain. I like the way they prick me when I'm moving around." Surgeons removed the needles at the same time as they repaired her broken arm and leg.

A PSYCHIATRIC SURVEY carried out by Wisconsin researchers into the reasons for nose-picking discovered that 0.4% of those surveyed did it for 'sexual stimulation'. Another 2.1% did it 'for enjoyment'. 65.1% used the index finger, 20.2% the little finger, and 16.4% stuck their thumb up their nose.

SALISBURY RESIDENT John Ulicsny, 35, was fond of hiding behind hedges and spying on women as they walked along a footpath. He always removed his clothing first, wrapped a butterfly-type metal coat-hanger round his waist, and tightened two neck-ties round the top of his legs to increase his arousal. He had apparently been gaining sexual satisfaction in this way for many years, until one day in 1994 when his coat-hanger became ensnared in a bramble bush. He fell headlong into the bush, scratching himself deeply, stumbled out in front of a woman walking her dog, then panicked and tried to hide by diving back into the bushes. That was where he was picked up by police. He was given a year's probation, and his hanger and ties were destroyed.

'MAD BOMBER' Erwin Mikolajczyk shot six people dead in March 1994, including the judge and his ex-girlfriend, then blew up himself and the courtroom in Bonn, Germany, with a home-made bomb strapped to his body. He had been fined £3,000 for beating his former lover, but police couldn't figure out why he was wearing wellington boots at the time of his demise. Then they visited his home and discovered another 140 pairs of wellingtons hidden in the cellar. All were in bright colours – pink, green, violet, yellow – and each pair was a carefully labelled record of his sexual conquests, with a different woman's name and date attached. It seemed that the 39-year-old boilerman had bought a new pair for every new woman he pursued, wore them during lovemaking, and lined up the boots in his living room so he could imagine naked women wearing them. There was also a collection of shiny black rubber mackintoshes in a bedroom.

AN ISLAMIC FUNDAMENTALIST in Egypt was quoted in 1992 as arguing that the sale of zucchini and eggplants should be banned. He claimed that both vegetables were stuffed with rice, usually by women, and that the stuffing process led to arousal.

JUST BEFORE THE FIRE that demolished part of Windsor Castle in 1992, a caretaker there was arrested for performing an undisclosed sex act with a jar of Bovril in the same chapel in which the conflagration began.

AN UNNAMED AMERICAN would habitually shoot himself while sexually aroused. He wore a bulletproof vest, but sometimes it wasn't enough to prevent quite serious wounding. He kept using less protection to get his kicks because he was building up a tolerance, and after receiving medical treatment on several occasions, he was ordered into therapy.

AN AMERICAN SOLDIER was reported to have a fetish for biting the heads off Barbie dolls at the point of climax and swallowing them. At one point an X-ray showed six of the heads in his stomach. He was said to re-use the doll's heads after a good boiling.

STEVEN BROWN of California had a fetish for getting his girlfriend to slap a pie into his face at the point of ejaculation. After she dumped him, he began to gatecrash social functions, inviting women to pie him in the face while he videoed it.

TWO UNUSUAL CASES of auto-erotic fatalities using power hydraulics appear in our files: in both cases the men were using the hydraulic shovels on tractors to suspend themselves for sexual stimulation. First we have the 42-year-old who was obsessed with his tractor to the point of calling it 'Stone' and having Christmas cards made up with a picture of himself and Stone upon it. While suspended upside down from the shovel, he accidentally hanged himself.

The other case concerns a 62-year-old who would hang upside down suspended by his feet from a backhoe, wearing only stockings and six-inch high heels. One day the support broke and the bucket dropped, crushing him to the ground and suffocating him.

Worlds of Fantasy

If a sex fantasy is the stuff of dreams, what are we to make of the following tales, where dreams become real to the dreamer, and it's only a fantasy to everyone else? And what happens when dream and reality rub up against one another?

TERENCE MIKOCH, 31, was arrested when the United Airlines plane he was travelling on arrived at Los Angeles in 1987. Apparently this was not where the Canadian-born geologist had expected to arrive, as he was under the impression that he was on a spaceship bound for another world: a spaceship, moreover, that was crewed by androids. And being androids, of course, it really didn't matter what anyone did to them, did it?

One of those 'androids' was stewardess Carol Cheney, who was making coffee in the galley when Mikoch grabbed her from behind, fondling her breasts, thighs and buttocks. She hit him with a coffee-pot filter and broke free, after which Mikoch, with a "wild, deranged look on his face", dropped his trousers and exposed himself.

The plane's captain confiscated Mikoch's passport and

noted that he was "cold to the touch", but half an hour later he again grabbed the same stewardess and jabbed her breasts with his fingers. Mikoch, who had a history of mental disorder, was cleared by the Los Angeles court, but told to get psychiatric help.

DR STRANGELOVE was the name police gave to Professor Tom Lippert, the man with the electric sex-machine. Like something out of a mad-scientist B-movie, the 25-year-old business lecturer at a Minnesota college had built the machine in the basement laboratory of his New Ulm home in 1975, assisted by 21-year-old Harold Tenneson. The next step was to find a guinea-pig.

Blonde student Susan Cochrane, 21, advertised for a lift home and accepted an offer by phone. Lippert and Tenneson picked her up, produced a revolver, forced her to drink a bottle of whisky, then drove her, bound and gagged, to the professor's home. Lippert, of course, was a man of honour who'd never force his attentions on a woman; but he was quite prepared to use his electric love-machine to make her fall in love with him.

The men carried Susan down into the professor's basement, donned white coats and assembled an array of apparatus. They wrapped her in a sheet and strapped her to a board, after which Lippert spent an hour explaining his passion, before she was unstrapped and shut in a box full of electric wiring.

Lippert pulled the switch, but nothing happened: he'd forgotten to plug in the machine. This was fortunate, as he then realised that the voltage was too high, and his victim would have been killed.

Even so, Lippert kept Susan prisoner under threat of death for a month, warning her that if she tried to escape her family would suffer. She was allowed to phone her family to tell them she was alright, which she was, as Lippert hadn't touched her. The nearest he got was one night in a storm, when he made her sleep with him; but then he simply lay for hours beside her with his clothes on.

Finally, Lippert and Tenneson found a low-voltage generator, strapped Susan in the box again, and threw the switch. She felt a faint tingling, but no love for the professor. And before the men could try the experiment again, the FBI turned up, having traced Susan's phone-calls to her worried family. She was released unharmed, while Lippert and Tenneson were taken to jail to face kidnapping charges.

AN UNNAMED WOMAN took newscaster John Suchet at his word in 1992, travelling from Manchester to London and turning up at ITN's building 10 minutes before he was due on the air one evening. She told reception staff: "I have an appointment with him at 5.40pm". A check of the records showed that Suchet had concluded the previous night's bulletin with the words: "We'll bring you up to date at 5.40pm. Join me then." Apparently thinking he was talking just to her, the woman had turned up for her romantic tryst.

A SOCCER-MAD WIFE in Austria became obsessed with her country's World Cup football star Hans Krankl in 1978. Named only as Annemarie, the 30-year-old woman built an altar in her bedroom before his life-size portrait, put fresh flowers in front of it every day and lit two candles, before adoring him in the nude. When she refused to make love with her 40-year-old husband Erwin unless he prayed as well, he sued for, and was granted, a divorce.

THERE MUST be something about Walt Disney characters.

In 1990, Californian Gary Carliss, 32, was planning to sue Disneyworld for "alienation of affections", saying his wife had fallen in love with the cartoon character Goofy. He claimed that she acted like a giggling schoolgirl when Goofy hugged her at Disneyworld, then went wild buying Goofy T-shirts, statues and posters. He added that on returning home she just walked round the house purring: "Isn't Goofy adorable?"

Rather more bizarre was the 1992 case of the unnamed 32-year-old woman with a long history of paranoid schizo-phrenia. She became convinced that Donald Duck had told her of his love for her via her neighbour's satellite dish. She was eventually found sitting in the satellite dish masturbat-ing, under the impression that the cartoon duck was making love to her.

Out Of This World

From aliens to genies, mermen to devils, all inhuman life is here, and it wants to have sex with us. And then there are those folks who resort to magic for sexual purposes...

PANIC SWEPT THROUGH LAGOS, the capital of Nigeria, in October and November 1990. Men going about their usual business were stopping to look anxiously into their pants or feel their crotch, and keeping an eye out for mysterious strangers who were said to be roaming the bustling streets and markets. The strangers were thought to be evil wizards who could instantly dematerialise a man's private parts, usually after shaking hands or some other slight bodily contact when they asked for directions. The missing items were said to turn up in a thriving witchcraft market, where they sold for hundreds of pounds.

Within a week of the rumours starting, the nation was in the grip of hysteria. A riot broke out in Enugu when a man boarding a bus shouted that his penis had vanished. The man in front of him was dragged off the bus and beaten.

Fearing a lynching, a policeman fired warning shots, but only made matters worse by killing the bus driver and badly injuring a woman and her child. During this period, four suspected sorcerers were beaten to death, and stories circulated that women's breasts were being stolen too. Yet although dozens of suspected organ thieves were attacked, no one was actually found to have lost his tackle, nor did any of the missing goods actually turn up in the markets.

GENDARMES were said to be grinning as they filed a report from a farmer in Tout, France, in September 1977. He said that he couldn't believe his eyes (and it seems the gendarmes didn't believe him either) when a UFO landed in his field in broad daylight. Then, apparently, a man and a woman, both naked, leapt from the UFO and made love three times before clambering back aboard and zipping off into the sky. The farmer tried to get nearer, but was hurled back by a 'blast'.

ABDUL MALIK, head of an Islamic boarding school in central Java, denied getting two schoolgirls pregnant in April 1989, saying it was the work of evil spirits. Police were called to the school after reports of prayer meetings to ward off the malevolent spirits, and Malik rejected a police summons to explain the pregnancies. He threatened to turn his own 4,000 evil genies on anyone who questioned his morality.

A SIMUNYE WOMAN from Swaziland took advantage of her husband's absence on a weekend trip to entertain her lover at her home. After a bout of lovemaking on Friday 4 December 1992, the couple fell victim to the condition known locally as *likhubalo*, which translates as 'dog-knotting' or 'love-lock'. Yells for help went unheeded, and it was not until the Monday morning that a woman neighbour discovered them. The naked duo were being taken away on a single stretcher by police when the husband met them on the road. Suspecting his wife's infidelity, he had cast an *ulunyoka* spell, which had caused the 'dog-knotting'. The ritual involves opening a pocket knife which, if not closed with the proper charms, locks the lovers together until they die. The husband agreed to perform the releasing ritual.

IN SWAZILAND, residents around the Ngwempisi River were convinced in 1991 that a merman had abducted six women when they went to the river to wash clothes. They were said to have already given birth to merchildren sired by him. Two Jewish prophets, Simanga Mthalane and Adries Diamini, announced an underwater rescue bid, vowing to eschew black magic. The rescue was called off after one prophet suffered a nosebleed and the other became feverish.

IN MOMBASA, Kenya, a man narrowly escaped being lynched by a mob in 1993 after he was discovered in bed with his neighbour's wife. The owner of the house, suspecting his wife, had obtained herbs from a sorcerer and administered them to her without her knowing. He then left the house in the morning, returning in the afternoon to find the house locked from inside. With his neighbours' help he broke in, to find the couple glued together. The husband only agreed to administer the antidote after negotiating a fine to be paid by the adulterer's family; but his neighbours wanted to burn the couple, as the adultery had taken place during the Islamic holy month of Ramadhan.

A FATAL ATTRACTION occurred in Lagos, Nigeria, in 1992. An adulterous couple was found locked together and dead on the floor of the husband's battery-charging shop. Police believed that during the lovemaking the woman had accidentally touched a live wire, fatally electrocuting them both; but more informed opinion (or rumour) spoke of blood and a worm oozing from her lover's mouth, the sure sign of a *magum* spell that fatally locks unfaithful lovers together.

RAMLAH BINTI MAT, a 48-year-old woman living at Kampung Perlis, near Balik Pulau in Malaysia, already had one son, aged 6. Becoming pregnant again, she claimed to have carried her second child for 13 months. In June 1977, she went to a clinic at Ayer Puteh, where a nurse confirmed she was pregnant, but a doctor told her she would have to have an operation, whereupon she became scared and kept away from him. On 17 February 1978, she went into labour, at which point her baby was stolen from her by an Orang Bunian, an invisible forest elf. She described the elf as a woman dressed in white and wearing a yellow shawl, who circled round her three times, placed a cold kiss on her cheek and then took away the baby. A neighbour said she saw Ramlah in labour, but didn't see the baby being delivered, and no one else saw the forest elf. The next night, the baby was apparently brought back for Ramlah to breast-feed it, and then taken away again.

Weird Tales

Human behaviour can be so odd that there are some tales which just don't fit into any category. Strangeness abounds in this round-up of miscellaneous madness...

THE CASE OF THE SEX-CRAZED Sunday-school mistress first came to light in 1981. The unnamed woman was outwardly a respectable spinster: tall, very thin, bespectacled and with greying hair; yet she couldn't resist a compulsion to pounce on men in a lonely lane. Feeling she was ugly, she hid in a hedge at night and waited for her victims to leave the local factory, with the result that she had five illegitimate children by men whose names she didn't know. Eventually she was referred to a Harley Street specialist, who put her on a course of hormone injections. The treatment was successful and she gave up lurking in hedges and went back to Bible classes. She then began shoplifting instead, to the complete confusion of all concerned.

Obviously believing in more direct action was the

woman of 73 who was prone to ambush young men as they walked in the woods near Vilnius, Lithuania. She was arrested in May 1994 for forcing men to strip and have sex with her on 20 different occasions.

OTHER FEMALE RAPISTS include the three young women, all in their mid-twenties and smartly dressed, who in 1990 offered a lift home to a 27-year-old man one snowy December night in Guelph, Ontario. Getting into the car, he found himself confronted by two blondes, a brunette, and a pistol. They drove the man to a secluded spot, stripped him and then, keeping him covered with the gun, took turns "committing sexual acts with him". Concluding their business, they drove off and left him lying exhausted in the snow.

Also in Canada, we have the tale of Maurice Conway, raped by his Filipina cleaning woman at the age of 74 in July 1987 while he was recovering from a stroke. He went to bed with a headache, found the maid snuggling up beside him, whereupon he says she "worked on me till I ejaculated and became exhausted". The maid wanted a Canadian child so she could claim immigrant status, and succeeded in getting pregnant, although she didn't contact Conway again until four years later, when she needed his support with immigration officials. Discovering he was a father, Conway went to court to gain visiting rights to the child, only to find himself ordered to pay $300 a month maintenance. He refused, saying: "I'm raped, why should I pay?"

AN ELEMENTARY-SCHOOL TEACHER and three other men were arrested on a golf course fairway in North Little Rock, Arkansas, in March 1993. They were standing in a circle masturbating, and didn't stop when first approached by an undercover police officer. They were still at it when he returned later with his partner to make the arrest, and they wouldn't stop then either.

GRANT OLIVER, 25, was fined £80 in October 1989 for using threatening behaviour likely to cause harassment, alarm or distress... to a blow-up rubber sex-doll. More than a little drunk, he was punching and shouting abuse at the doll in Torquay when spotted by police, and refused their invitation to stop. The cops then proceeded to arrest both Oliver and his doll, putting the doll in the front seat of the car and putting her seat-belt on, then locking them up together in a cell to sleep it off. Oliver said that the worst part of the affair was explaining to his wife the next morning.

ALSO DRUNK was Mervyn Lilburne, 39, of Ballarat, Australia. He was fined £200 in 1991 for obscene exposure and damage after trying to have sex with a park statue; the damage was caused when he fell into a flowerbed after people started shouting at him.

WHEN TWO MALE CUSTOMERS happened to pass the manager's office in a department store at Falkenberg, Sweden, in December 1990, they found that the door had accidentally been left open. Glancing inside, they were startled to see a girl undressing through a lit-up window. One of the men recognised her as his own girlfriend, so they went in and discovered they were looking into a changing room. One of the changing room's mirrors was transparent, giving the manager, Kaj Bergquist, a full view of everything that went on. He claimed he was only trying to prevent shoplifting, but ended up having to resign anyway.

IN SIBERIA, a 30-year-old woman identified only as Margarita found a novel way of beating the Russian economic crisis in 1991. Her apartment in Krasnoyarsk had a balcony overlooking the exercise yard of a labour camp, so, at 100 roubles a time, she began stripping for the prisoners. Inmates in the compound threw bundles up to her balcony containing money and instructions on when she should go through her routine; she made up to 6,000 roubles a month in the summer. The average Russian wage at the time was only 300 roubles. However, the Siberian snow put an end to her work. "In winter it gets cold on the balcony," she explained, "and the windows freeze so they can't see anything through the glass."

IN ONE of those tantalisingly brief news reports which fail to go into detail, we hear that in a 1989 court case at Dorchester a woman accused her husband of making her take part in kinky sex games with white mice. The case was halted when the ladies' toilet exploded. Oh to know more...

SPANISH ROMEO Jose Cado of Valencia promised to marry 12 different girls in 1978. Unfortunately, they all met each other when every one of them turned up to pay a motoring fine on his behalf. They also discovered that every single one of them was called Anita, after which the fighting started. As police parted the infuriated ladies, Cado made a run for it, and left town.

IN ITALY, 40-year-old Carmelo Baglo suffered three years of frustration. Every time he tried to make love to his wife Anna, 38, she burst into song, usually operatic arias. As she simply lay there on her back, stared him in the eyes and sang at him, he found his desires vanishing completely. She was unable to explain why she did it, simply saying that "sex makes me burst into song". Finally unable to take it any more, in 1991 he beat her up. He was charged with grievous bodily harm.

WHEN DEFENDING a man charged with sending obscene books through the mail in 1991, a lawyer in Wisconsin phoned the prosecution attorney and asked to see the offensive material. It arrived at his office the following morning... by mail.

SOUTH AFRICAN DOCTORS in the town of Maseru were trying to help 34-year-old salesman Morris Adams in 1994. His problem was that he was allergic to pretty women. Every time one came near him, he'd break into a sneezing fit.

IN DURBAN, South Africa, an unidentified bird-man was prosecuted in 1977 for repeatedly buzzing a back garden where a blonde was sunbathing in the nude. As the hang-glider pilot flew overhead he shouted: "I'd like to sleep with you!" The outraged woman tried to hit him with a broom, but he was out of reach.

IDENTIFIED ONLY as 'Manuela', a 13-year-old schoolgirl gave birth to a baby boy in a village near Weilheim, Germany, in 1980. No one believed her claims that she knew nothing about sex and had never had a boyfriend, but doctors confirmed that she was a virgin. Even so, villagers shouted abuse at her in the street, and she was forced to leave school. The mystery was solved only a week before she gave birth, when her mother's lover, Richard Weh, 37, was discovered tip-toeing into the bedroom of Manuela's younger sister in the middle of the night. He confessed that nine months before he had sneaked into Manuela's room and "played about" with her, though she had remained fast asleep all the time. He said he hadn't got beyond sexual foreplay, and had made sure she was a virgin when he left her, but he was jailed for rape anyway. The baby was adopted.

A COUPLE were invited to buy an inflatable sheep sex-aid after answering a newspaper advert for rechargeable batteries. They received a personally addressed mail-shot headed 'Luv Ewe', quoting a price of £17.95. A drawing was accompanied by a description: "She has been developed after years of research into how to bring the joy of sheep into your love life without the obvious problems of real sheep. No bleating to alert the neighbours. No risk of ruining your prize lawn." When the couple complained, it proved impossible to contact the firm.

CHAPTER TWENTY-ONE

Is There Sex After Death?

The answer seems to be yes. From posthumous exhibitionism to necrophilia to randy ghosts, the end of life doesn't seem to be the end of sex

POLICE BATTLED with sightseers and TV cameramen in 1983, all of them eager for a look at 37-year-old oil heiress Sandra West, from San Antonio, Texas. This wasn't surprising, as her only attire was a lace baby-doll nightie, and she was sitting in her Ferrari sports car. What was perhaps surprising was that this was her funeral, and Sandra was about to be buried next to her husband. Unfortunately, whatever ideas Sandra might have had about the good times to come in the next life were rather spoiled by the local authorities, who insisted that at the last minute the Ferrari had to be placed inside a wooden crate, and that two truckloads of cement had to be poured into the grave to discourage vandals.

IN SPITE OF COMMUNIST PRESSURE on such ancient customs, a "ghost marriage" took place in China's Shandong

115

province at the end of 1982. The wedding was typically Chinese: guests, gifts, piles of food and many bottles of wine, and trumpeters to herald the bride's traditional journey to the bridegroom's home. In this case, though, that home was the local graveyard, because both the wedding's major participants were dead.

The wedding was arranged by the girl's parents after she had been killed in an accident, to prevent her suffering the shame of being a spinster in the afterlife. A matchmaker was hired who found a suitable husband in a recently deceased youth, whose sister acted as a go-between, taking a dowry of food, wine and cigarettes to the bride's father. Then the girl's body was exhumed and reburied next to her husband's tomb, at the same time that the wedding was celebrated.

In what might seem an excess of zeal, another Chinese "matchmaker for the dead" was arrested in February 1992 after carrying a woman's corpse on an eight-day journey. He dug it up in Sichuan province and carried it 750 miles to Shanxi, where it was to be buried with the body of a co-worker's brother, who had died without marrying.

FROM CHINA'S HUNAN PROVINCE comes the tale of Xie Zhanbei, who committed suicide by drinking pesticide in January 1994 after being criticised by his father. But Xie's relatives blamed his 19-year-old widow, Luo Xianglan, for his death, beating her, stripping her and making her sleep with Xie's corpse. Xie's sister and sister-in-law took his corpse and "forced it on top of Luo Xianglan and made her kiss it and sleep in the same bed with it". The original report hinted darkly at "further, more serious abuse" of the widow, although what that might imply is a matter of conjecture.

IN CALIFORNIA, Archie Calvin Whitehurst, 29, broke into a convalescent home in Fremont in 1994 and sexually assaulted the corpse of an 83-year-old woman. He pleaded guilty to a count of burglary when the case came to court, but claimed that the corpse had consented to sex. However, the charge of attempted rape was dismissed, as California has no statute to criminalize the act of having sex with a dead body. He was sent to jail for seven years, with psychiatric treatment recommended.

INCONCEIVABLE though it may seem, necrophilia cases do occasionally have a happy outcome. In 1992, an 18-year-old Romanian girl, declared clinically dead, regained consciousness while being raped on a slab by a Bucharest mortuary attendant. Police arrested the shocked necrophiliac, but the girl's parents refused to press charges because their daughter "owed her life to him".

THE MOST ANCIENT CORPSE to be involved in a potential case of modern necrophilia is that of 'Otzi', the 5,000-year-old man found in a glacier in the Italian Alps. Shortly after he was found, 10 women came forward and asked if they could be inseminated with his sperm.

FROM THE LIVING who seek sex with the dead, we turn to the dead who seek sex with the living. Tales of phantom fondlers are commonplace enough, and the tale of the Hallam family of Normanton, Notts, is typical. Beginning in June 1975, Peter and Mary Hallam, along with children Rebecca, 21, Frances, 16, and Tom, 13, began to notice their 16th century farmhouse was haunted. The male Hallams saw the ghosts of an elderly couple, while another ghost, said to be a light in the shape of a man, reserved his attention for the ladies. After merely sitting on Mary's bed, he became rather more intimate with her daughters.

Frances, just going to sleep, heard heavy breathing; then the sheets were lifted and 'someone' got into bed beside her and put his arm round her waist. The phantom feeler then slid down the bed and left at the foot. Rebecca also heard heavy breathing and sighing, but the ghost remained outside the covers, pressing down on her feet and thighs, feeling like an animal crawling up the bed. She also had her bottom slapped in broad daylight. Strangely, the phenomena seemed to peak at the full moon.

MORE CURIOUS is the tale of Bob Williams, landlord of the Old Vic pub in Basingstoke. In 1979, 24-year-old Bob found himself sharing his bed with a female ghost, though he wasn't 'the object of her affections. He simply heard her heavy breathing and sighing, but saw and felt nothing. "It's as though there is a woman lying next to me making love," he said. "She sounds a very passionate sort of woman." Bob hid his head under the bed-clothes until the panting stopped.

STORIES OF spectral consummation are rather rarer, but we have the following tale of 20-year-old Jenny Price of Birmingham who, in 1978, was claiming complete satisfaction with her ghostly gallant. Although the family had known about the ghost for years, it seems that Jenny had not been told about it. It first made approaches to elder sister Lorraine, but it merely touched her shoulder. Then, when she was 17, Jenny was sitting up in bed one night when she felt invisible hands round her neck. With great strength, the hands pushed her down on the bed. She tried to scream, thinking the ghost would strangle her, but soon realised he had other intentions. After that she was scared to go to bed in case the attack was repeated, which it was, a week later. She soon realised that the ghost meant her no harm, however, and started looking forward to his visits, which began to take place as often as three times a week.

By the time three years had passed, the biggest problem seems to have been how to get Jenny out of bed, she being too intent on staying there waiting for her invisible lover to show up. It began with a kiss on the shoulder, then hands slipped under the covers to caress her before he got into bed beside her. "I just let him do what he wants," she said, "and he does it beautifully... he certainly can love."

Eventually Jenny's mother Olive, 50, decided she wanted to get in on the act too, so she swapped beds with her daughter for three weeks (what her husband Trevor thought about this is not recorded). However, the randy wraith didn't show up; he preferred blondes, apparently. Still, Olive didn't think anything immoral was going on. She'd talked it over with the vicar, and he'd told her that ghosts probably don't bother with morals...

FAR MORE UNNERVING were the rash of tales from Uganda at the beginning of 1995, headlined 'Strange ghosts on raping spree?' Invisible forces were said to grab the victims, tear off their clothes and have forceful intercourse, and women and girls were reported to be hurrying home at night, although as the ghosts were most prone to operate after dark and seemed able to pass into buildings quite easily, there seemed little logic in this. From Makerere University it was reported that a ghost had attempted to rape a girl in the Africa Hall, but only got as far as ripping off her blouse and skirt.

A more circumstantial tale came from Ruhoko village in Kabarole district, where a ghost in the form of a man apparently raped the 12-year-old daughter of Mutabazi Jack on 17 January. She was returning from a family party at about midnight when she met a man in a black suit who she didn't recognise. He grabbed her, carried her to a nearby bush and raped her. While this was happening, some 'force' apparently prevented her from speaking and moving, and she was only able to do so when her attacker disappeared, as suddenly as he had appeared in the first place. In hospital, the girl insisted that it was a ghost who had attacked her, rather than a real man.

IN 1990 it was realised that a large number of male Thai workers in various countries round the world were dying of a mysterious illness, labelled 'Sudden Unexplained Nocturnal Death Syndrome'. Most of the victims were from north-east Thailand, where similar deaths had been reported in the past, and by April of that year a panic was sweeping the region. Those most likely to suffer the disease had their own theory about its cause. Many men started painting their fingernails red and putting on women's sarongs before going to sleep, to deceive murderous female spirits, called *Pi*, whom they believed were ghost-widows on husband-hunting sprees. In this way they hoped to fool the sex-starved spirits into thinking they were female and so avoid their clutches.

References

REFERENCES

INSIDE FRONT COVER
Friend of the Earth: *Sun*, 19 Feb 1993. *Wolverhampton Express & Star*, 25 April 1995.

CHAPTER 1: EMBARRASSING ACCIDENTS
Staffs policeman: *D. Star*, 12 Jan 1995. Zagni: *S. Express*, 26 July 1987. Deijk: *People*, 18 Dec 1994. Swindon man: *People*, 5 March 1995. Bristol man: *D. Mirror*, 4 Dec 1987. Middlesex man: *Evening Standard*, 12 Dec 1979. Melbourne man: *D. Star*, 11 Aug 1979. Schneider: *Western Mail*, 8 Nov 1989. Essex man: *D. Mirror*, 27 Dec 1990. Israeli letters: *S. Mirror*, 14 April 1991. Newman: *D. Telegraph*, 14 July 1992. California man: *D. Record*, 23 Oct 1992. Gillingham woman: *Sun*, 6 July 1990. Tupper: *Eastbourne Herald*, 7 May 1994. Cheuvront: *D. Star*, 21 July 1994. Hooper & Healey: *Times*, 3 Aug 1994, etc. Meyer: *Wolverhampton Express & Star*, 9 May 1994. Hague man: *Canberra Times* (Australia) 21 Dec 1991. Puanmuangpak: *Japan Times*, 15 Aug 1993. New York man: *New York Times*, 3 June 1988. Vacuum injuries: *British Medical Journal*, 5 July 1980. Vacuum death: *Mensa Bulletin*, Jan/Feb 1995. Pennsylvania man: *Medical Aspects of Human Sexuality*, July 1991.

CHAPTER 2: THANKS FOR THE MAMMARIES
Texan women: *Atlanta (GA) Constitution*, 15 Sept 1989. Roberts: *D. Mirror*, 19 April 1985. Hess: *NY Post*, 12 April 1994, etc. Henri: *D. Record*, 7 Nov 1994. Plympton driver: *Sun*, 27 May 1987. Salisbury robbers: *The Scotsman*, 16 Sept 1986. Cologne robbers: *Victoria (BC) Times-Colonist*, 19 May 1988. Dutch robbers: *NY Post*, 7 June 1994, etc. Thai transvestites: *Reuters wire*, 29 Dec 1992. NY subway: *AP wire*, 1 Sept 1994. Marek: *Western Mail*, 28 May 1994. Wilcox: *News of the World*, 2 May 1993. Austin barbers: *Beaumont (TX) Enterprise*, 25 July 1985. Hillendahl: *San Francisco Chronicle*, 25 Feb 1977. Syracuse mother: *Washington Post*, 30 Dec 1992. Li Xiaomo: *E. Standard*, 2 March 1984.

CHAPTER 3: TACKLE TALES
Mussika: *D. News*, 18 Dec 1993. Rahman: *Singapore Straits Times*, 13 Aug 1994. Cincinatti surgeon: *Sun*, 18 June 1992. Yorkshire tattoo: *Guardian*, 4 April 1990. Chinese hoaxers: *D. Post*, 21 Dec 1988. Miller: *D. Record*, 4 Aug 1994. Munich man: *Sun*, 23 Jan 1995. Kenyans: *AFP wire*, 7 Oct 1992. Forti: *D. Record*, 22 Dec 1994. Adelaide woman: *Reuters wire*, 30 April 1991. London woman: *Guardian*, 20 Jan 1995. Germans: *D. Star*, 20 April 1994. Brindley: *Sun*, 11 Feb 1986. Israeli: *Victoria (BC) Times-Colonist*, 28 Nov 1994. Shanghai surgeons: *Sun*, 7 May 1986. Chan Tze-tan: *D. Star*, 9 Feb 1995. Irian Jaya: *People*, 24 April 1994. Lopez: *Diario* (Madrid) 29 Nov 1992. Spurtyn: *UPX wire*, 27 May 1995.

CHAPTER 4: BOBBITTED
Chinese wife: *Guardian*, 19 Jan 1994. Cambodian woman: *Shropshire Star*,

REFERENCES

21 Oct 1985. Gillett: *Washington Post*, 22 Jan 1994. Cox: *D. Telegraph*, 18 March 1982, etc. Okech: *Sun*, 19 Oct 1986. Fortuin: *D. Telegraph*, 3 Sept 1981. Malaysian man: *Playboy*, April 1983. M62 man: *Middlesbrough Evening Gazette*, 27 Sept 1986. Samanci: *Reuter's* wire, 17 Aug 1991. Kampioni: *D. Star*, 18 Feb 1994, etc. Destry: *D. Star*, 6 Oct 1994. Baker: *D. Record*, 14 July 1994. Italian biter: *Independent*, 11 Feb 1995. Zappala: *E. Standard*, 31 Oct 1983.

CHAPTER 5: A WALK ON THE WILD SIDE
Hamilton: *Evening Post*, 20 Oct 1986. Hernandez: *St Louis Post-Dispatch*, 27 Aug 1987. Daugherty: *Atlanta Journal & Constitution*, 21 Sept 1990, etc. Chei Fui: *S. Express*, 6 July 1984. Tipton: *D. Mail*, 2 Feb 1989, etc. Gomes: *Guardian*, 25 Feb 1993, etc. Mohapi: *Guardian*, 29 July 1986. Cornbury: *D. Telegraph*, 28 Feb 1989. Alger: *D. Chronicle*, 10 April 1908. Khan: *Leicester Mercury*, 12 Aug 1992. Smallwood: *D. Mirror*, 20 Feb 1990. Flockton: *D. Mirror*, 4 Dec 1987. Nottingham mugger: *People*, 11 Sept, 1988. Paton: *D. Record*, 27 July 1992. Chinese sisters: *Reuter's* wire, 3 Feb 1993. Chinese sex-swap: *Reuter's* wire, 24 July 1992. Newman & Willis: *Independent*, 30 April 1994. Berkowitz: *D. Star*, 7 Feb 1981.

CHAPTER 6: FLASH HARRIES (& HARRIETS)
Johnson: *Holborn & City Guardian*, 28 Dec 1984. Gill: *S. Mirror*, 30 Nov 1990. Minneapolis man: *San Jose Mercury News*, 23 June 1992. Pugh: *Sun*, 23 May 1986. De Notte: *D. Mirror*, 19 July 1990. Corby cyclist: *D. Telegraph*, 23 March 1987. Biassa man: *D. Express*, 1 Aug 1988. Ward: (Darlington) *Northern Echo*, 27 Jan 1987. Gipsy Joe: *Western Daily Press*, 23 July 1992. Morales: *Duluth News-Tribune* (Minn.), 22 May 1988. Los Angeles woman: *Houston Chronicle* (Texas), 12 April 1989. Ronda men: *D. Star*, 17 March 1994. Israeli girl: *D. Express*, 2 Sept 1983. Catena: *D. Mirror*, 20 Feb 1992. Fransen: *Coventry Evening Telegraph*, 3 March 1994. Hampshire woman: *Sun*, 21 Jan 1988. Burnham woman: *News of the World*, 12 March 1989. Bonn man: *People*, 9 Oct 1994.

CHAPTER 7: OUT-OF-CONTROL BIRTH-CONTROL
Colombian theft: *South China Morning Post*, 23 Jan 1992. Aborigine song: *S. Mirror*, 21 Oct 1973. Quandong: *Times*, 28 Jan 1988. Swedish IUD: *S. Mirror*, 17 March 1974. Kurdish IUDs: *Independent*, 7 Aug 1990. Skadeland: *AP* wire, 13 Oct 1993. Dutch vasectomy: *Reuter's* wire, 4 Sept 1992. U534: *D. Record*, 28 Sept 1993. Leroy Grant: *D. Record*, 21 March 1993. Damien Stuart: *Brisbane Courier Mail*, 17 May 1995. Lino Missio: *Guardian*, 28 May 1994. Chinese children: *Bangkok Post*, 4 July 1992. Philippines TV: *Times of Malta*, 19 March 1994.

CHAPTER 8: MARRIAGES MADE IN HEAVEN (AND HELL)
Arnold G.: *S. Express*, 21 Oct 1984. Ogoun: *B.T.* (Denmark) 17 Oct

REFERENCES

1990. Sichuan man: *Victoria (BC) Times-Colonist*, 4 Nov 1990. Mangyan women: *E. Standard*, 22 March 1984. Indonesian man: *Berita Harian*, 17 April 1981. Rao: *Independent*, 24 Aug 1993. Mezquita: *D. Star*, 4 Feb 1994. Tek Kor: *St Louis Post-Dispatch*, 13 May 1985. Warden: *St Louis Post-Dispatch*, 9 Feb 1986. Sri Lankan man: *Weekly News*, 3 Oct 1987. Jiff: *D. Telegraph*, 5 Feb 1991. Nasution: *D. Telegraph*, 23 Feb 1981. Awang: *Gulf News*, 27 Feb 1988. Ray: *Providence Journal-Bulletin* (Rhode Island), 1 May 1986, etc. Jackson: *Guardian*, 29 May 1991. Omar: *E. News*, 14 Oct 1977. Fatehabad man: *Mail on Sunday*, 24 April 1983. Suldano: *The Voice*, 24 Nov 1984. Odessa woman: *Austin American-Statesman* (Texas), 16 Jan 1994. Hampshire man: *Sun*, 16 March 1986. Rangpur farmers: *AP* wire, 5 May 1995.

CHAPTER 9: BONKERS
Swedish taxi driver: *Halifax Evening Courier*, 21 Oct 1994. Henderson & D'Arcy: *D. Telegraph*, 7 Aug 1992, etc. Chatanooga schoolkids: *Guardian*, 2 June 1988. Israeli teacher: *Guardian*, 20 Dec 1979. Czech football fan: *D. Record*, 11 Feb 1994. Winter: *D. Mirror*, 5 June 1985. Toronto hotel: *St Louis Post-Dispatch*, 18 May 1990. Reading couple: *D. Star*, 4 May 1994. Celle woman: *D. Star*, 30 June 1994. Washington: *D. Record*, 25 Sept 1992. Chong: *S. Morning Post* (Hong Kong), 22 Jan 1995.

CHAPTER 10: ONLY IN IT FOR THE MONEY
Moussali: *D. Mirror*, 24 June 1987. Bulawayo brothel: *Independent*, 9 Feb 1990. Beisvitz: *Arab News*, 15 Nov 1989. Stella: *S. Express*, 23 Sept 1990. Call-girl nuns: *D. Express*, 19 Feb 1988. Blot: *S. Dispatch*, 25 Nov 1928. Kuala Lumpur man: *Edinburgh Evening News*, 18 Sept 1992. Amsterdam prostitutes: *San Jose Mercury News*, 14 April 1995. Dutch sex: *Sussex Evening Argus*, 21 My 1994. Norwegian prostitutes: *D. Express*, 10 Oct 1988. Taiwanese grandmothers: *D. Telegraph*, 10 Aug 1993. Von Rutschmann: *D. Star*, 23 Feb 1991. Cowan: *Toronto Sun*, 15 Oct 1989. Brattleboro kids: *Houston Chronicle*, 8 Sept 1983. Los Angeles priestess: *E. Standard*, 12 Dec 1989. Luxembourg hotel: *Independent on Sunday*, 26 Feb 1995.

CHAPTER 11: DOCTOR, DOCTOR!
Brasschaat optician: *Portsmouth Journal*, 23 March 1995. Fisher: *Newsweek*, 23 Oct 1989. Whalen: *UPI* wire, ? April 1982. Clark: *Victoria Times-Colonist*, 25 Aug 1987. Louisiana surgeon: *D. Record*, 26 March 1994. d'Avis: *American Medical News*, 13 March 1995. Lee: *D. Mirror*, 9 Aug 1989. Sugameli: *S. Express*, 7 Oct 1984. Wood: *D. Express*, 25 Oct 1989. Jacobson: *D. Mirror*, 5 March 1992.

CHAPTER 12: PHONE-ICATION
Leigh: *Independent*, 2 July 1994. Olpe boy: *D. Mirror*, 22 July 1992. Pickess: *D. Telegraph*, 13 March 1982. Austrian student: *Atlanta Constitution*, 5 Nov 1992. Kazan: *D. Mail*, 16 Nov 1984. Cherry: *News of the World*, 17 Sept 1989. Fort Lauderdale hoaxer: *D. Star*, 3 Jan 1984. Kenneth Cohen: *D. Express*, 23 Aug 1984. Kah: *News of the World*, 6 Aug 1978. Mitchell: *The Record* (Hackensack, NJ), 3 Feb 1995.

REFERENCES

CHAPTER 13: BEASTLY TALES
Gripton: *Sun*, 17 Feb 1995. Hauge: *Sun* 31 Jan 1995. Hale: *Sun*, 7 Jan 1991. Sonepat ape: (Cleveland, Ohio) *Plain Dealer*, 19 Nov 1986. Romeo: *D. Telegraph*, 3 Feb 1992. Clarke: *S. Express*, 19 Sept 1982. Jeffrey: *Sussex Evening Argus*, 15 March 1994, etc. Tucson man: (Arizona) *Daily Wildcat*, 19 Sept 1994. Mugo: *Kenya Times*, 23 Nov 1993. Zimbabwe man: *Independent*, 2 March 1995. Talal: *Guardian*, 11 Aug 1981. San Antonio man: *San Antonio Express-News*, 28 May 1988. Smith: *Independent*, 27 June 1990. Howard: *D. Record*, 28 Sept 1992. Gronau: *S. Mail*, 11 Oct 1992. Perkins: *New Scientist*, 10 Nov 1990. De la Cruz: *S. Express*, 4 Nov 1990, etc. Tofts: Penguin Book of Lies, edited P. Kerr 1991, p.155. Irish red setter: *Guardian*, 22 May 1992. Gomez: *S. Times*, 26 April 1992.

CHAPTER 14: STRANGE PENETRATIONS
Gray: *D. Mirror*, 15 July 1993, etc. Swedish women: *Expressen* (Sweden), 10 March 1993, etc. Peterson: *D. Telegraph*, 8 Nov 1990, etc. Kelly: *NY Post*, 17 Nov 1994, etc. Burnett: *D. Mail*, 17 Sept 1994. Arbuthnot: *Guardian*, 5 Dec 1994.

CHAPTER 15: THOSE CRAZY JAPANESE
Knickers: *The Face*, Dec 1994. Vending machine: *Reuter*'s wire, 22 Sept 1993. Crackdown: *Washington Times*, 28 Sept 1993. Saliva: *Mainichi Daily News* (Japan), 8 May 1994. Sweaty underpants: *Observer*, 16 April 1995. Women's vending machines: *D. Record*, 31 Aug 1992. Yoshifumo Ito: *Liberation* (France), 15 July 1989. Samu Yamamoto: *Brisbane Courier Mail* (Australia), 3 Dec 1994

CHAPTER 16: THAT OBSCURE OBJECT OF DESIRE
Barnes: *D. Star*, 6 Oct 1981. Indonesian man: *Emirates News* (Abu Dhabi), 3 March 1986. Sneddon: *Toronto Sun*, 23 Nov 1980. Drogheda man: *D. Record*, 29 March 1988. Patterson: *Lancaster Sunday News* (Pennsylvania), 24 Nov 1991. Leonardo da Toenail: *D. Telegraph*, 20 March 1981 etc. Hunter: *UPI* wire, 1 June 1985. Pisa man: *D. Star*, 15 March 1994. St Louis man: *St Louis Post-Dispatch*, 3 March 1992. Hay: *D. Telegraph*, 4 Oct 1986, etc. Paris man: *S. Mail*, 12 July 1992. Brook: *News of the World*, 1 Feb 1981. Wright: *Guardian*, 13 July 1990. Banbury man: *D. Mirror*, 24 Aug 1968. Sparkhill man: *D. Express*, 27 Nov 1985. Goodhew: *Sun*, 23 Sept, 1989. Davidson: *D. Mail*, 29 Oct 1981. Kenyon: *D. Mirror*, 4 June 1975, etc. Malaysian man: *D. Express*, 11 Sept 1978. Dijon man: *D. Mirror*, 16 July 1969. Everett: *Scotsman*, 18 June 1985, etc. Guyer: *San Jose Mercury News*, 6 May 1992. Willshire: *Daily News*, 29 July 1927. Virginia Beach man: *Playboy*, Nov 1981. Milwaukee man: *Milwaukee Journal*, 18 Sept 1987. Los Angeles bus-drivers: *Boston Globe*, 12 Dec 1982. Symons: *News of the World*, 8 May 1988. Simmons: *D. Star*, 15 Dec 1993.

CHAPTER 17: COMING TO A CLIMAX
George: *Independent*, 7 Dec 1992, etc. Baker: *San Luis Obispo County Telegram-Tribune* (California), 3 Aug 1987. German major: *S. Mirror*, 23 Jan 1977. Debbi Anne: *Loaded*, Aug 1994. Knoxville boy: *AP* wire, 24

REFERENCES

April 1995. Amri: *Sussex Evening Argus*, 9 June 1993. Gay actor: *Sun*, 28 May 1990. Kleist: *Sun*, 20 Sept 1994. Nose-picking: *Journal of Clinical Psychiatry*, Feb 1995. Ulicsny: *Salisbury Journal*, 15 Dec 1994. Mikolajczyk: *D. Record*, 12 March 1994. Egyptian stuffing: *Newsweek*, 27 June 1992. Windsor caretaker: *Sun*, 5 Sept 1992. American gunman: *Vanity Fair*, Nov 1992. American Barbie-biter: *D. Star*, 22 Feb 1994. Brown: *D. Star*, 22 Feb 1994. Power hydraulics: *Journal of Forensic Sciences*, March 1993.

CHAPTER 18: WORLDS OF FANTASY
Mikoch: *Sun*, 3 December 1987. Lippert: *News of the World*, 6 April 1975. Suchet: *D. Record*, 29 Sept 1992. Krankl: *News of the World*, 23 July 1978. Carliss: *S. Express*, 16 Sept 1990. Donald Duck: *Irish Journal of Psychological Medicine*, Nov 1992.

CHAPTER 19: OUT OF THIS WORLD
Nigerian panic: *Independent*, 30 Oct 1990, etc. Tout farmer: *News of the World*, 25 Sept 1977. Malik: *Independent*, 14 April 1989. Simunye woman: *Guardian*, 9 Dec 1992. Swaziland merman: *Wolverhampton Express & Star*, 9 Oct 1991. Mombasa couple: *Kenya Times*, 8 March 1993. Lagos couple: *New African*, Oct 1992. Mat: *New Straits Times* (Malaysia), 19 Feb 1978.

CHAPTER 20: WEIRD TALES
Sunday school teacher: *D. Star*, 7 April 1981. Vilnius woman: *D. Mirror*, 16 May 1994. Guelph women: *D. Mirror*, 10 Dec 1990. Conway: *Victoria (BC) Times-Colonist*, 23 Feb 1995. North Little Rock men: *Arkansas Democrat-Gazette*, 3 March 1993. Oliver: *D. Telegraph*, 30 Oct 1989. Lilburne: *D. Star*, 20 June 1991. Bergquist: *Sydsvenska Dagbladet*, 2 Jan 1991. Margarita: *Reuter*'s wire, 24 Oct 1991. Dorchester mice: *D. Record*, 14 July 1989. Cado: *Reveille*, 24 March 1978. Baglo: *D. Record*, 14 Feb 1991. Wisconsin lawyer: *S. Mail*, 24 Feb 1991. Adams: *S. Mail*, 6 Nov 1994. Durban man: *Sun*, 23 March 1977. Weh: *News of the World*, 12 Oct 1980. Luv Ewe: *D. Telegraph*, 13 May 1992.

CHAPTER 21: IS THERE SEX AFTER DEATH?
West: *Weekend*, 17 Aug 1983. Shandong ghost-marriage: *S. Express*, 9 Jan 1983. Sichuan matchmaker: *Guardian*, 19 Feb 1992. Luo Xianglan: *The Herald* (Harare, Zimbabwe), 4 March 1995. Whitehurst: *San Jose Mercury News*, 6 July 1994. Romanian girl: *AFP* wire, 29 Jan 1992. Otzi: *Sun*, 19 July 1992. Hallam: *D. Mirror*, 7 Sept 1976. Williams: *S. People*, 4 Feb 1979. Price: *News of the World*, 26 March 1978. Uganda ghosts: *The Monitor* (Uganda), 6 Feb 1995. Thai workers: *Independent*, 17 April 1990, etc.

Welcome to the World of the Bizarre and the Bewildering

From UFOs, Bigfoot and visions of the Virgin Mary to weird tales and human oddities, Fortean Times is a respected chronicler of strange phenomena with 23 years' experience of reporting from wild frontiers. Informed, open-minded, sceptical, and above all extremely funny, FT has the low-down on what's out there.

A six-issue subscription costs £12,
a 12-issue subscription £24 in the UK,
including postage and packing.
Or send for a sample issue for just £3.
Just fill in the form below and return it to:

FORTEAN TIMES SUBSCRIPTIONS
FREEPOST (SW6096), SOMERSET BA11 1YA
CALL (44)1373 451777 FOR OVERSEAS RATES

☐ I would like to subscribe to Fortean Times for 12 issues (£24 UK inc p&p)

☐ I would like to subscribe to Fortean Times for 6 issues (£12 UK inc p&p)

☐ Please send me a recent sample issue (£3 UK inc p&p)

NAME _____

ADDRESS _____

_____

POSTCODE _____ TELEPHONE _____

☐ I enclose a cheque/International Money Order payable to: JOHN BROWN PUBLISHING LTD

☐ Please debit my: *(Circle one)* Visa Access Mastercard
American Express Diners Connect card

CARD NUMBER _____

EXPIRY DATE _____ SIGNATURE _____

We will accept photocopies of this form if you prefer not to cut your book. **AO301**